College Professoring

or
Through Academia with
Gun and Camera

by **OLIVER P. KOLSTOE**

Illustrated by Don Paul Benjamin

SOUTHERN ILLINOIS UNIVERSITY PRESS
Carbondale and Edwardsville

Feffer & Simons, Inc.
London and Amsterdam

Library of Congress Cataloging in Publication Data

Kolstoe, Oliver P
 College professoring.

 1. College teaching. I. Title.
LB2331.K57   378.1'2   75–1237
ISBN 0–8093–0710–3
ISBN 0–8093–0712–X pbk.

Contents

Introduction

Some time ago, the Board of Trustees was considering some new personnel policies for our university. As chairman of the Faculty Research and Publications Committee, I was obliged to prepare a position paper for the committee detailing the probable consequences of the policies. The proposed regulations appeared so obviously unworkable that I found myself doubting the seriousness of the board. I could not believe the policies were not presented as a practical joke. Correspondingly, my paper was written tongue-in-cheek as though the whole procedure was some huge mistake and not to be dignified by a response which considered the regulations anything other than funny. Since such a paper was not suitable to be presented in open testimony, I had to prepare a more restrained one; but this left me with some excellent material and no place to use it. Since I tend to brood about any waste of literary effort, I began to explore possible alternatives to simply discarding it. Careful considerations of other aspects of college life led to the recognition that boards of trustees were not alone in practicing the absurd. College faculties made their contributions also, but these were usually not well known outside of college circles. As I began to detail some of these peculiarities, I shared them with some of my graduate students and colleagues who unfortunately laughed. No one of only moderate strength of character can withstand that kind of encouragement, so I continued my writings until they grew into a book-length manuscript.

In the course of the presentations, often someone would say, "Can't you just see some poor professor trying to become famous, or trying to figure out how to teach, or trying to get the secretaries to type his work or. . . ." It finally dawned on me that the material might lend itself to cartoons, so I asked Don Paul Benjamin, who as University ombudsman continually deals with college absurdities, if he would like to convert some of the material to a visual form. He did, with results most pleasing to me.

The selection of a title was another problem. I wanted something which was descriptive of the content, most of which is true as well as being slightly comical, so it had to be both descriptive and different. "College Professoring" seemed to fit those requirements. The subtitle was frankly purloined from a friend. In 1972, I had a book on mental retardation published. At a convention a few months later, Professor Thomas E. Jordan greeted me with, "How is 'Through Mental Retardation With Gun and Camera' going?" The description seemed much too apt to be simply allowed to be lost. I appropriated it and I thank him for it. Dr. John Wilcoxon did editorial surgery.

Finally, the book does an injustice to thousands of women who are competent practitioners of college professoring. I apologize to them and particularly to my wife, Dr. Betty Jean Kolstoe, an accomplished college professor in her own right. But since the vast majority of professors are male, and since my graduate students are preponderantly male, and since the stereotype of the college professor is male, this book is written from the viewpoint of a male chauvinist; albeit a benign one.

Oliver P. Kolstoe

Greeley, Colorado
July 1974

College Professoring

1 *On Being a College Professor*

EVERY YEAR some thirty thousand people earn academic doctoral degrees. For most of them, that degree is the ticket needed for admission to the land of academia. Not all of them choose to live in that wonderland and, of course, not all who wish to be chosen, are. For the degree only makes one eligible —it is not a guarantee of admission. To get in, one must meet and pass various other tests. Without the degree, however, most people don't even meet the eligibility requirements for being considered for inclusion or exclusion.

Just to be able to participate in this process, one must have persisted in the role of student through four years of an undergraduate program of uncertain usefulness, at least a year of master's level work, and generally not less than three years of doctoral work including the planning, preparation, presentation, and defense of an original piece of research which will quite probably never be looked at by more than a few loyal friends or spiteful colleagues.

One can legitimately question the judgment of anyone who would demonstrate such singlemindedness of purpose, particularly when the financial rewards which attend this enterprise are exceedingly miniscule compared to the remuneration of colleagues in medicine, dentistry, and law. We must sup-

Considering the land of academia

pose, therefore, that the noneconomic rewards will more than compensate for the lack of material wealth, because some rational factors must be found which can explain why reasonably intelligent people would take up college professoring as a lifetime occupation.

There are some 2,550 institutions of higher education in this country. They range in programs from those with two-year associate degrees to those with extensive post-doctoral offerings. There may be as few as one or two hundred students, as in some private colleges or as many as 40,000 or more, as on the campus of the University of Wisconsin in Madison. The intellectual climate may vary from the sterility of some church-sponsored colleges, whose mission is quite frankly indoctrination, to ultraliberal universities whose attempts at indoctrination are spoiled by the impossibility of one person teaching all the classes in a given department. It should be obvious that if the professor is of the same persuasion as the small college, it is a most comfortable place to teach, but the educational opportunities are considerably better in the larger institution where each professor's influence is diluted by his colleagues' offerings. The optimum institution, where a professor can be influential but students may still be exposed to several different points of view, probably does not exist; but the ideal of the optimum institution persists as do all myths sustained by the eternal optimism of mankind and a small kernel of truth. For elements of influence and differences are present in varying degrees in nearly every school and indeed constitute one proof of the contention that there is a remarkable sameness in all institutions of higher education. People do choose to become college professors because they wish to exert some influence and because they enjoy being surrounded by exciting differences which can almost be guaranteed to be present in whatever school one may select. For many, the exciting environment is of such value that it is a bargain compared with more material things offered as rewards in other business or professional enterprises. When it comes to choosing between them there is no contest. Aca--demia wins. Professors consider it better to have a stimulated soul than a bulging warehouse.

Although technically there are differences in institutions of higher learning — colleges, universities, schools, and multiver-sities — unless one strives for precision, the terms are often used interchangeably. Of course they are not synonymous. A department is a section within a university, college, or school which gives instruction in a certain field. A school is a group of departments which specialize in a particular branch of learning. A college is a collection of departments and/or schools which provide instruction in related fields. A univer-sity is a collection of departments, schools, and colleges. It usually encompasses both general and professional or special-ized fields of learning. A multiversity is a name coined to describe several universities which share an uncomfortable marriage with a single governing board and are related by legislative parentage. Departments, schools, and colleges have a venerable history and tradition. Multiversities are a product of twentieth-century American know-how with neither his-tory nor tradition to guide them. Only recently has it come to the attention of the academic community that bigness is not necessarily related to goodness. Of course we have known for a long time that neither is littleness, nor any other sizeness for that matter. Quality is independent of quantity; a fact not fully gathered by many boards of governance and other legis-lative groups, but one which enables perceptive professors to select where they will labor without being swayed by size.

Just as the professor expects to exert an influence on the institution with which he is associated, so also does he expect the institution to exert an influence upon him. He expects the institution to support and facilitate his scholarship so he will, over a period of time, get better — hopefully, become the best in the world in his field. It is here that quantity and quality become confused. To become the best a professor needs to be surrounded by extensive library holdings, elaborate laboratories, highly specialized equipment, and intelligent if not brilliant colleagues, all held together by an administration which values his potential contribution to knowledge more than efficient material management systems. Any institution which prizes the ease with which faculty activities can be audited over the ease with which faculty can pursue knowledge richly deserves its reputation as an academic fumble factory. Unfortunately, in order to justify extensive libraries, laboratories, equipment, and faculty most universities seem to think that a substantial number of people have to be available to use the facilities. Therefore, there is often a relationship between the size of an institution and its quality. Big and good go together. Furthermore, the presence of a philosophy of administration which facilitates faculty scholarship is extremely rare. Most professors find, however, that being left alone is often as good as and sometimes better than being helped. Again, the advantage goes to larger rather than smaller institutions. However, in the interest of fairness, it is only honest to suggest that this condition stems from the inordinate difficulty of any administrative officer in keeping up with the activities of a large and energetic faculty, not from any deliberate administrative philosophy. Since administrative offices are chronically understaffed they must spend their time in committee meetings discussing how to do an impossible job with insufficient manpower. This condition leaves professors free to do as they see fit and must be considered one of the world's biggest boons to scholarship. Thus, the desire to pursue scholarly interests, ideally with institutional sanction and support but at the very least with a minimum of institutional interference, looms as a major reason for choosing to become a college professor. Most professors prize freedom to pursue their scholarly interests above all other employment conditions: security, titles, and money. Not that these are unimportant, they just occupy a lower priority position than freedom.

In the past ten years recorded knowledge has expanded

Administrative offices are chronically understaffed

more than in the preceding one hundred years. In those one hundred years knowledge expanded more than in the entire four thousand or so years of recorded history. It is no mere coincidence that higher education has undergone an expansion in direct proportion to the knowledge explosion. According to histories more than ninety percent of the discoveries which have made modern civilization possible have either their roots or their actual origins in the ivory towers of academia. This should come as no surprise to those who are acquainted with higher education. First of all, there are about eight hundred thousand extremely well-trained professionals available to search for new things. This would be a formidable group if it existed alone. But in addition to this army, is a second backup force of graduate students; bright, energetic, creative, and without sufficient experience to recognize insurmountable obstacles. Therefore, they are able to pursue knowledge like the man from LaMancha pursued evil. It would be most surprising if no knowledge came from these efforts. Second, promotions and salary determinations, while not necessarily directly related to scholarly activities, certainly are among the more identifiable contingencies. Therefore, not only are the faculty able to satisfy their own needs for scholarship in the institutional setting, but it is easier for administrators to promote and raise the pay of faculty who have a record of research and publication than to try to explain to them that they should not be doing what they have been trained to do. Particularly is this true when the public information officer of the institution takes every opportunity to publicize any article, book, or pamphlet authored by staff members, thus demonstrating that this indeed is what they are supposed to do. Third, college professors know a great deal about the fields in which they work. It is axiomatic that the more one knows about something, the less certain he is about his knowledge. In this situation, curiosity reaches a high peak, and the result is further exploration of the subject, usually from a new and

Publishing is one of the things professors are supposed to do

Tenure encourages professors to explore the world of ideas

different viewpoint. There is no need to particularize that whatever is found out will be useful, edible, salable, or even interesting to others. It is enough to add one more bit of knowledge to that handed us by our predecessors, for this is the function of scholars. Businesses which stand or fall on profit cannot afford to support very many people whose function is to be curious enough to try to find out about things which may not be very closely related to the product or service of the company. Yet the company and the rest of society itself is vitally dependent upon accurate information. It has to come from somewhere, and colleges have come to serve that purpose. This is where security plays a significant role. Society has great need for the information and discoveries which come from scholarly work. Yet scholars cannot afford to be held accountable for the immediate usefulness or popularity of their ideas — these must stand on the verdict of history (essentially the scrutiny of other scholars). The university setting therefore is ideally suited as a dwelling place for untried ideas. Some institution has to exist which is apart from the mainstream of functioning society where magnificent mistakes as well as magnificent discoveries can be made without jeopardizing the individual who makes them or the society which supports him. The fact that ninety percent of the discoveries have come from institutions of higher learning makes it obvious that the chances of producing useful ideas are very high. Such odds would be acceptable to any red-blooded all American bettor and apparently are acceptable to taxpayers also. In any case, the mechanism which provides the scholar with the security to try the untried is tenure. Tenure essentially guarantees to the college professor that (except for conspicuous drunkenness and flagrant immorality) he is encouraged to explore the world of ideas with no concern for their practicality. This is a heady experience of limitless possibilities and one which appeals to the Walter Mitty in each of us. Most college professors would rather pursue exciting possibilities than

Most college professors would rather pursue exciting possibilities than humdrum realities

humdrum realities. The desire to deal with what might be rather than what is emerges as a compelling force for choosing to become a professor.

The need for accurate information which society must have to function at all, let alone efficiently, makes it mandatory that college professors worship the credo that honesty is the best policy. It is not just the best — it is the only acceptable policy. Around this need has developed the whole procedure of the "scientific method of research." The purpose of publishing scholarly papers is to allow other scholars to duplicate exactly the author's work. This is validation by replication and is the only acceptable method of determining fact. If another professor can find no confounding element in a procedure used by another professor and if following the procedure produces the same results, then the results obtained are labeled facts. A fact is, above all, dependable. Facts allow planning, organizing, and managing — the very life's blood of an industrial society. Facts are exciting to discover and dreadfully dull afterwards. To college professors there may be few things more exciting than discovering facts or more pedestrian than dealing with facts. In the excitement of the pursuit, there is a strong incentive to publish those procedures and results which lead to the tentative indentification of facts. The publication, however, is going to be very carefully examined by colleagues who are nearly as expert, probably just as bright, and equally capable of jealousy as the original author. Any dishonesty, deceit, oversight, omission, or camouflage will be instantly detected with quick reprisal in the form of shattered credibility for the author. There is probably no greater price than can be paid than the loss of professional integrity. For this reason, professors tend to be scrupulously honest about their work. This is not to be confused with modesty, but often is. When a professor describes the limitations of his work, he is simply beating others to the punch. It is so hard to be modest about doing something no one has done before that most professors don't even try. They simply accept that people who are modest have a great deal to be modest about but that people who discover new things do not. Thus there is a premium on honesty, not modesty. Furthermore, members of the business world often follow the credo "caveat emptor" (let the buyer beware), which permits camouflage and omission, if not downright deceit, since it is left to the consumer to detect that he is being had. Not so in academia. It is the obligation of the discoverer to identify exceptions and shortcomings before they are pointed out by gleeful colleagues. It is probably this mandate to honesty which makes college professoring attractive to many. It is wonderful to be virtuous in an otherwise sinful world — particularly when it does not cost much to be pure and hurts a lot when one is not.

2 On Being Hired

TO BECOME a college professor one must be hired for a college or university faculty. Such a simple statement is considerably more involved than it appears on the surface. Not many years ago a chronic shortage of professors existed which seemed unlikely to be eased. Not so at present. With the advent of the Nixon administration, federal funding both for research and for service programs was sharply curtailed. In addition, the National Aeronautics and Space Agency programs were continued on a very limited basis, thus releasing thousands of highly trained engineers, physicists, and mathematicians. The resulting decline in the national economy made it increasingly difficult for parents to support their children in college at the same time that work opportunities for students from federal programs became fewer. These forces resulted in colleges with fewer students, less federal research money, cancelled service projects, reduced legislative support, alumni gifts restricted by an uncertain economy all surrounded by a climate of distrust inherited from the hippy culture willed us by our California colleagues. As a consequence, the present supply of potential professors far outstrips the demand. Far from being unusual, this condition more nearly approaches the norm. Historically there have nearly

The present supply of potential professors far outstrips the demand

always been more professors available than people have really needed. This time, however, the influence of modern technology has brought order to the colleges and universities as they try to decide how many professors they need in the form of the full-time-equivalent student statistic or F.T.E. In the past, the need for faculty was apt to be decided on the basis of gaps in expertise. For example, if it appeared that computers might rule the world and if a college had not enough professors to staff all the courses needed to teach computer science, then a new faculty member with expertise in computers would be recruited. Subsequent deaths, retirements, and susceptibility to pirating from other schools also removed experts from departments. They were replaced by persons of comparable competence or, in the absence of demonstrated ability, promise. Thus it was common practice to attempt to hire students of outstanding or at least well-known professors in the hope that some of the professor's expertness may have rubbed off on his students. The way to assure oneself on being hired as a college professor was to become a student of some well-known professor in a currently popular field. In the sciences and social sciences cults of disciples developed around the great names associated with popular theories, and it was from these pools of talent that potential professors were drawn.

That was the condition of the past. Now the determination of need is based on an exceedingly complex formula involving student F.T.E. A full-time-equivalent student is one who enrolls for an average load (usually fifteen hours of class work per week) during any given term. Through the medium of consensus judgment (probably divinely guided) it has been determined that each level of instruction, freshman through advanced graduate, requires a different investment of a faculty member's time and is assigned a different F.T.E. value. Likewise, each kind of instructional approach; lecture, seminar, tutorial, or laboratory, also has a different F.T.E. value. The resultant score for each teaching assignment is the number of hours of credit times the level F.T.E., times the instructional F.T.E., times the number of students. Since each faculty should generate 1.0 F.T.E. then it is easy to determine which departments are carrying their fair share of the teaching programs and which ones are not by applying the formula to each faculty member in the department and getting the total for the department. The beauty of the system is that it can all be put into a computer and the computer makes the decision as to which areas are overstaffed or understaffed and which professors are overworked or underworked. Thus administrators are saved from having to make decisions which have to be defended. Because of this, it seems likely that the practice will persist for sometime.

Obviously, the way to beat the system is to generate more F.T.E. than an average of 1.0 per professor. Since the level F.T.E., the instructional F.T.E., and the number of credit hours are relatively fixed in the formula, the only element that can vary much is the number of students enrolled. Large classes generate more F.T.E. than small ones, therefore, the more students you can pack into a class, the more the total score for the class, and the better the department work-load looks. When budget time comes around, new faculty positions can be allocated to those departments with the greatest work-load record as determined by the computer and once again the administrators do not have to take on the unpopular task of being administrators. Furthermore, when the total F.T.E. of the class, professor, department, school, or college is divided into all of the instructional costs for each class, a cost/effectiveness ratio can be calculated so it is possible to determine just how much it costs to provide each student a unit of education. This can be incorporated into annual reports which go to legislators and other boards of governance who then can know exactly what an education is worth. Once again, the system serves to demonstrate that bigness and goodness go together.

Fortunately, quality is still independent of quantity. Thus,

Allocations of faculty positions are made with computer printouts of F.T.E.

while allocations of faculty positions are being made with computer printouts of F.T.E. and cost/effectiveness ratios, decisions about whom to hire are still made on the basis of expertness needed and the best prospect for becoming an expert gets the nod. As has always been the case, initially the student of the well-known professor still has the best chance. But being identified as a likely prospect for a position is only the first step, albeit a giant one. Next comes the testing.

The reputation of any department depends upon a great many things, but by and large the dominant factor is faculty expertise. Since each person in the department is assigned some reflected glory from his colleagues, it becomes paramount to field a team of individual and collective experts. When a person of acknowledged mastery of an area leaves, the reputation of the entire department may be seriously endangered unless the replacement is conceded to be as good as or shows promise of equaling (surpassing) the late replaced. Initially, then, every effort is made to secure a replacement with stature at least as great as the departed. This is usually done by telephoning persons known to the members of the department. This starts with oblique references like "do you know anyone who . . ." and finally get around to "you wouldn't consider joining us out here in God's country would you?" The invitation is never extended directly nor in such a way as to suggest that one institution is superior to another, but instead emphasizes some irrelevant fringe benefit. It should come as no surprise that God's country is always wherever the invitation is made from.

Obviously, many established people will move when properly approached, but just as obviously there are not enough experts to go around, so a good many departments have to look for promising but unproved graduate students. At this point departments go to great pains to protect themselves from precipitous selection. First, a careful job description is prepared. Typically, this includes the academic degree re-

Every effort is made to secure a replacement with stature at least as great as that of the departed

quired, certification, licensing or registration, what experience is required, probable faculty rank, the personal characteristics desired, salary range, job responsibilities, courses to be taught, and contract period. Then a committee is formed to circulate this information to college and university departments which are believed to have reasonably respectable training programs. When inquiries begin to come in, the committee asks discreet questions about candidates of faculty acquaintances on the candidate's home campus. These are always by telephone so no one can later prove subterfuge, libel, or misrepresentation, for these are the three choices available to the respondents. Complete candor is neither possible nor really expected. The result is a rather incomplete discription of the candidate's abilities, because the respondents can talk only about what they know and they typically are not well enough acquainted to offer much authoritative information. This leads to the next step, personal inspection.

Personal interviews are generally conducted at the expense of the employing institution for the simple reason that candidates are too poor to afford the cost of visiting. A more subtle reason is to protect the institution from any obligation, real or imagined. A fundamental concern is the fear of buying an unknown package and jeopardizing the reputation of the whole department. In order to assure that no one person must accept full responsibility for a poor choice, the democratic process is scrupulously observed. For example, the candidate who is invited to be interviewed is one who has been ranked high on the list of potentials by members of the department after they have made discreet phone inquiries and carefully compared the personal and professional records revealed in the vita sheets and confidential letters of recommendation from the university placement centers. The principle which governs this procedure is called "share the blame." In a further extension of this democratic practice, arrangements are made to allow each member of department about fifteen minutes in

A fundamental concern is the fear of buying an unknown package

The junior faculty probably have only one or two published things and they are very conscious of them

which to probe the knowledge depth of the prospective faculty member. Needless to say, in such a short period of time it is difficult to get much beyond "Did you have a nice flight?" and "What do you think of my latest article?" The candidate who emerges from this trauma with the fewest negative points is the one who had a lousy flight and says so (this establishes empathy with all other faculty, each of whom professes to abhor flying) and who made it a point to read the latest publications of the *junior* members. The probability is that the really senior professors have three or four things which either just came out or are about to so they can't remember which is the latest anyway. The junior faculty, on the other hand, probably have only one or two published things and are very conscious of them. The clincher, however, is that there are very few senior professors compared with the number of nonsenior faculty. In a democracy, you put your energy where the votes are.

Final interviews are with the members of the administrative hierarchy: deans, provosts, vice presidents, and presidents. Generally, the smaller the institution the more important is the opinions of these administrators; probably because in small schools the chances of administrators encountering junior faculty in day-to-day activities is fairly high. In large institutions the administrators are better insulated from faculty so they apparently feel safe in allowing faculty to select their own colleagues. The candidate would do well, however, to remember that there are exceptions to every rule, so it pays to be cautious until after one is hired. In the final interview, the administrators take care to explain the conditions of employment should a contract be offered. Any dickering to be done takes place at this point because neither the university nor the candidate is committed. Even if a tentative agreement is reached, the commitment is still limited to the candidate, but the door has been closed to any further negotiation.

Almost never is a contract offered a candidate while he is

still on campus. In fact, the host campus usually doesn't even go so far as to suggest a serious interest. For some strange reason, any declaration of interest is completely unilateral and consists of extracting a pledge from the candidate that *if* a contract were proffered, it would be accepted. Once again, the reason for this practice goes back to the time honored ploy by faculty of blackmailing administrators with offers from other institutions into granting undeserved salary raises. The fact that no such blackmail could possibly be levied by an unhired faculty does not interfere with the studious adherence to the procedure. There are right and wrong ways to do everything, and in academia form will be followed even when it is patently absurd.

If the candidate agrees that *if* a contract for a certain salary, for a specified period of time, and describing certain work requirements were offered, he would be pleased to consider joining the faculty of the university, the matter is considered consummated. Since these commitments are verbal and carefully couched in "if" terms, each party then adds a disclaimer. The university essentially says that all the conditions are subject to the wishes of the Board of Trustees. The candidate essentially says that all the conditions are subject to the wishes of his equivalent to the Board of Trustees, his wife. In such a climate of apparent indecisiveness it is a wonder anyone is ever hired. It should be remembered, however, that in academia things are seldom what they seem. What appears to be irresolute behavior is really just a restatement of the continuing firm stance that everything that can be done to protect the institution from taking a precipitous action which might jeopardize the reputation of the school will be done. The "well it seems okay, but . . ." response of the candidate simply signals that he is not going to risk his reputation by accepting a job in a school which will not facilitate his professional development. Mutually protected, the administrator and the candidate can then go their respective ways, secure

In such a climate of apparent indecisiveness it's a wonder anyone is ever hired

in the knowledge that each has fulfilled his obligation in an exemplary manner.

With no strings to hobble them, each can now go about solidifying the commitment. The hiring official usually polls the faculty in the department for their reactions. If he gets a positive vote from the faculty, he then will solicit opinions from the administrative hierarchy. This has two effects: first, it gives the administrators a voice in hiring practices thus furthering the illusion of importance which surrounds the office, and second, it alerts them to the fact that a contract will soon be coming to their desks and they will have no reason to hold it up because they have already approved the candidate. This effectively cuts down on bureaucratic red tape, thus allowing the institution to be very efficient in matters which are fairly unimportant. The important part of the hiring procedure, evaluating credentials, weeding out the undesirable candidates, and interviewing the top prospects, can then be allowed to function in an incredibly inefficient manner. So long as efficiency is identified with one part of the operation the whole procedure is generally credited with that virtue and no one will question whether it is efficient or not. In academia we protect our illusions as fiercely as we do our reputations.

After the contract has been given a positive vote by the Board of Trustees, it is sent to the candidate for his signature. In the meantime he has been busy telling his wife and her relatives that the offer he is being made is a rare opportunity to become associated with an institution with an international reputation and that after all, money isn't everything.

Neither argument actually has much validity. Being a member of the faculty of an institution of some fame is no guarantee that any of it will rub off on you. Fame is something achieved through extremely hard work over a considerable period of time; it accrues to individuals, not institutions, and it is nontransferable. More important, money is one indication of the value placed on your services. The critical aspect is not

In academia we protect our illusions as fiercely as we do our reputations

Being a member of the faculty at an institution of some fame is no guarantee that any of it will rub off on you

necessarily how much money you are paid; rather it is how rapidly you can improve your salary through promotions and raises. If the possibility of doubling your salary in ten years is not nearly certain, then you may want to reconsider plans for staying very long. Phrased differently, if the beginning salary for an assistant professor is $10,000 the beginning salary for a full professor should be $20,000 or more. Raises should be between nine and ten percent per year. This rate of increase can truly convince your family that the beginning salary isn't everything. It is the future that counts. Armed with this attitude of faith in the future, you are well on your way to making the most of your employment because you know you will be able to earn raises which are substantial enough to be noticeable — to actually have the effect of raising your standard of living, not just raising your morale, to allow you to live better, not just feel better. Annual raises go a long way toward helping you in the pursuit of happiness. And this is certainly one of the principle reasons why you decided to become a college professor in the first place.

3 *On Conditions of Work*

ONE MAJOR difference between professionals and other people is the individuality of the employment conditions for the professional and the uniformity of employment conditions for the nonprofessional. Because each college professor has his own contract, he is considered a professional. It is at this point that professionalism is stretched pretty thin, for the contracts offered have a sameness which borders on the identical. To be sure, some contracts are for the nine-month academic year and some for twelve months; some contracts are terminal and some continuing; some lead to tenure and some do not, yet all of them deal with the same subjects. If a person is an instructor, his salary will be at the same level as other instructors with similar experience and training. If he is on a full-time basis, the number of hours per week he is required to teach will be the same as other instructors on a full-time contract. Office hours, student advisement, research assignments and committee responsibilities are generally expected of all faculty so they are often not specifically written into the contract. If they were, they would all look alike. Each person gets a different contract but it is just like everyone else's.

It is difficult to understand why the form of professionalism is treasured when there is so little substance to it. While it is

Contracts often have a sameness which borders on the identical

true that many university faculties have surrendered their professional individual contracts for unionized common agreements, the number of schools so affected are few. The trend, however, is unmistakable. Unionizing of faculties and collective bargaining are becoming more common and may yet sweep the country. Soon that symbol of professionalism, the individual contract, may disappear. Even if it does, it is quite likely that employment conditions won't change much. anyway.

Fundamentally, college faculties are hired to teach. Since most universities have at least eighty-five percent of the student body made up of undergraduates, it is obvious that the greatest probability is that new faculty will teach undergraduate classes and more than likely, the correlational law of newness will apply. This law states that "news" attract. Actually, they don't; it just looks that way because new students are assigned to the newest instructors. It would probably be better to invent a new law which states that "news" are easier to manipulate than "olds."

This is closer to the truth, but still lacks complete validity. It is perhaps more honest to recognize that the overriding principle of protecting the reputation of the department at all costs probably is the deciding factor in faculty assignments. Since new faculty are not yet sufficiently well-known for the older members of the department to be sure whether they will add polish or tarnish to the reputation, it is prudent to assign them to activities which have little effect on the departmental reputation. Freshmen are equally untried and singularly uninfluential. Therefore, if the new instructor is not very good as a teacher, from thirty to seventy percent of the freshmen will flunk out anyway, so not many people who will grow up to be alumni are going to be affected. The new faculty member's potential to damage the reputation of the department is effectively minimized. In the happy circumstance that he turns out to be an acceptable teacher, it is good experience to learn to

New professors are easier to manipulate than old professors

field the naive questions of freshmen before being thrown in to the big leagues with upperclass majors and graduate students. Furthermore, since multiple sections of classes are offered at this level, the new person can be assigned two sections of the same class. This makes multiple preparation unnecessary and allows more time for his own research or other scholarly activities, thus providing him the opportunity to establish himself as a contributing member of the department and enhance the departmental reputation. Furthermore, during the second and third years of teaching, the instructor will be repeating classes previously taught. Student evaluations can be acted upon so the instructor can concentrate on strengthening the areas in which students found him weak without having to completely organize his class notes from scratch.

In the event that the university has a system in which a faculty member must demonstrate that he is qualified to teach graduate students, the assigning of new faculty to lower-division courses has an additional function. In many schools, no one may become a member of the graduate faculty until he has a record of publication of independently conducted research. Typically, dissertations prepared during doctoral work do not count. It is necessary, therefore, that the new professor collect some publications in scholarly journals. Just the mechanics of publishing takes a great deal of time, so any kinds of time-saving activities are well worth embracing. Quite often these universities use a kind of apprenticeship program before the new professor earns the right to sponsor doctoral students as major professor and guide the students' dissertation preparation. By being allowed to serve on student doctoral committees, the fledgling professor can observe the old hands guide the student through his course work, his comprehensive examinations, and the planning, executing, and defending of an original dissertation. By the time his own research has been published, the department has a pretty good idea of whether he is capable of taking the responsibility for

Professors are not generally considered non-things

shepherding one of his own students through the maze to a doctor's degree. Even when the evidence leads to a positive decision, the department can still hedge by assigning one of the senior professors to the committee, just in case. It seems a little incongruous that in an institutional climate which so highly values the taking of risks in exploring ideas, there are almost infinite precautions taken to protect the departmental reputation while exploring the potential of some of the most highly trained people in the whole world. Apparently, risks in academia are confined to non-things. At least it is of some comfort to realize that professors are not generally considered non-things.

Even course-time assignment has its protective side effects. Generally, any course is scheduled to fit the work schedule of the professor who teaches it. Thus, the courses are spaced during the day and throughout the week so they will not overlap each other. Furthermore, administrative efficiency dictates the use of university classrooms and laboratories evenly throughout the same time period. Someone has to see to it that about the same number of courses are offered at eight A.M. as are offered at ten or two or four. Since senior professors are apt to have university commitments such as faculty Senate at four on Mondays or Research Committee at three-thirty on Wednesdays or some such other meetings, they are given the opportunity to select times (and sometimes classrooms) first. Since the professors are just as susceptible to concern for creature comfort as anyone else, they tend to schedule their classes according to convenience. The prestige required to rate this kind of differential treatment is not inconsiderable. For this reason, the classes taught by these academic stars are often among the more sought-after classes. Given an equal chance, students pick the classes of the proven professors, leaving the unproven for, at best, second choice. Once again, albeit not wholly by design, the least convenient times generally are manned by the newer staff members and the fewest

Casual visitors to the department will most often encounter the novices rather than the pros

students (relatively) take classes at those times because classes offered at the more popular times fill up and are closed to further enrollment first. If a professor's prestige is really outstanding, he may even have the privilege of setting his own enrollment limits. But barring this, he may accomplish the same thing by selecting a room for his class which holds only so many students. The desire for these kinds of privileges often drives otherwise nonpenurious professors toward eminence. Among the many effects of these practices, not the least is the instruction of the fewest students by the newest instructors and the subsequent lesser likelihood of loss of departmental reputation. Prudence, again, triumphs.

There are other consequences of this condition, not all of which are completely salutary. Because the newer professors have classes scheduled at inconvenient times, they are apt to start the teaching day early and end late. Furthermore, they are more likely to be teaching every day rather than concentrating their classes into two or three days per week. As a consequence, casual visitors to the department will most often encounter the novices rather than the pros. Students also will find it easier to contact the new faculty than the old. The departmental image at a local level, therefore, may often be projected by these encounters and suffer accordingly. However, since most departments are much more concerned with national than local fame, this may be considered an extremely low price to pay for the other advantages enjoyed.

An advantage for the new professor's which may more than compensate them, is that being around the department all day every day brings them in close contact with departmental secretaries. Unfortunately, secretaries are subject to great hassling by everyone—students, faculty, administration, and the public at large. They are on duty every day from eight to five and have no place to hide from the unpleasantnesses which attend any office. It requires uncommon grace to explain to an irate parent that Professor Cadwalader missed his

Secretaries have no place to hide from the unpleasantnesses which attend any office

No acceptance by the secretary means you may have to type your own letters

appointment with them after they had just flown two thousand miles to discuss the *D* grade of their daughter, because he is cooling his heels in the Dean's office while the Dean waits to see the vice-president who is waiting to see the President who is trying to explain to a member of the Board of Trustees whose daughter got a *D* from Professor Cadwalader, the circumstances under which capital punishment is possible. Being available to take visitors who want to see absent senior department members off the hands of the harried secretaries goes a long way toward achieving secretarial acceptance. It is worth a great deal for a new faculty member to be accepted because the degree of acceptance dictates the priority which governs office work. No acceptance means you may have to type your own letters. Acceptance means you may sometimes have your work done before some of the senior members of the department. The occurrence of such an event is often considered of even greater moment than getting promotion or tenure and is certainly more rare.

4   *On Faculty Work Load*

SOMEHOW COLLEGE PROFESSORS have never worked by
the hour. This custom probably had its roots in the middle
ages when scholastics were all men of God residing in monas-
teries. As these havens for scholarship took on the functions
of colleges during the age of enlightenment, the search for
knowledge and understanding continued to be viewed as a
labor of oneship with God, and revelation was considered to
be a legitimate outcome of this relationship. Time constraints
could scarcely be imposed by man on God since He obviously
had his own plan and time schedule for letting man in on the
secrets of the universe. Man correspondingly, if he were going
to receive revelations, had to be available when God was. And
man, being a creature of no mean ingenuity, just as likely
found it useful to be available to God during uncommon times
of the day; particularly if he did not wish to have his labors
interrupted by trademen, students, parents, administrators,
and fellow scholars. It is also quite probable that the more
intense his work became, the less he wanted it interrupted,
the more important it probably was and the more uncommon
the working hours became. Furthermore, productive scholars
have always put in a perfectly horrendous work week. It
should come as no surprise that people who are quite bright

and who work many hours turn out to be more productive than equally bright people who don't work either as hard or long. Because of this, the work habits of these peculiar but productive people came to be respected by other people even though they were not fully understood.

In the course of time, as a ruling class began to develop among the European tribes, princes and kings became aware that the information they got from scholars was often more dependable than that obtained from theologians. Since the problems of government were rooted in the real world of day-to-day living, they turned more and more for information (not necessarily advice) to the investigators of the secular rather than the purely spiritual world. Furthermore, they found that information from scholars was necessary to the training of their own children in the art of ruling their worldly kingdoms. While they may have turned to theology for divine guidance, they turned to scholars for methods of getting their alternative routes, what to expect when they got there, and possible consequences of the journey.

It was during these years and the developing eighteenth and nineteenth centuries that support for universities and subsequent control moved from the exclusive hands of the church to the state. It is doubtful, though, that administrators appointed by kings were any more successful than administrators with God's backing in regulating the working hours or the interests of scholars. Fundamentally, administrators are neat. They seem to like to maintain orderly schedules in the institutions they manage. The scheduling of programs, classes, staff, secretaries, janitors, meetings, and reports are often of greater importance than the contents of these things. Furthermore, despite monumental protests to the contrary, administrators are better equipped to deal with quantitative data than qualitative. They tend to find it easier to count how much or how many rather than to try to determine how good — unless good is considered synonymous with rare, in which case they

Fundamentally, administrators are neat

are dealing with how many anyway. In this regard, they are more closely related to the managers than scholars. Indeed, even though college presidents, chancellors, provosts, vice-presidents, executive officers, deans, associate deans, assistant deans, and chairmen are nearly always chosen from the academic ranks, their functions are to regularize rather than to facilitate scholarship. As such, administrators are always the enemies of academics. Fortunately, it is usually not a bitter feud because the chief function of a university is still the pursuit of knowledge, and this fact is recognized by administrators fully as much and perhaps even more so than by academics. A consequence of this condition is the striking of an uncomfortable compromise between administrators and scholars which pleases neither perfectly; so it is, therefore, workable. This agreement recognizes that creative work knows no time constraints. Therefore, the right of scholars to set their own working hours subject to the dictates of no one is strictly observed. This pleases the scholars but not the managers. In return, professors are required to teach a certain number of hours per week. This satisfies the administrators and is tolerated as a profound but necessary nuisance by the professors. Thus a delicate balance is struck between the professor's accountability to the institution and to the scholarly discipline which enslaves them. Their work load is an extended tightwire act between the two.

With the colonizing of America a new era dawned for the college professor. To be sure, early American colleges were church-supported institutions designed to train men of the cloth to minister to the spiritual needs of the new world, and college professors were primarily concerned with divine revelation, but Thomas Jefferson and his hoodlum friends soon changed all that. As they attempted to transplant a ruling plan from abroad it immediately became evident that the serf-master pattern from Europe could only work where people were prevented from moving to another spot if they became

The faculty work load is an extended tightrope act

discontented with their present habitations and conditions. Where unclaimed land was freely available, people could not be controlled. This precipitated a revolution from which evolved a concept of government never before attempted: government with the consent of the governed. Among the many consequences foreseen by Jefferson's genius was the absolute requirement of a universal system of education so the governed would understand their government well enough to know when to and when not to consent — when to retain the governors and when to throw the rascals out. From this recognition arose Jefferson's own University of Virginia and the proud academic traditions which soon spread to state-sponsored schools in other places.

While the growth story of American universities may be fascinating, the function story is our concern, for there arose communities of scholars who were not responsible to kings, princes, popes, bishops or even presidents or governors. They were responsible to the people, not to the government. The tools of scholarship and the energies of the scholars could be turned loose on every aspect of life. In return for this carte blanche the scholar was expected to communicate his discoveries to his employers with only occasional advice on how to best use the information discovered. In return for a relatively small amount of time spent in teaching, not only were scholars granted the right to use their other available times when and as they saw fit, but they were granted the right to study whatever interested them. Never in the history of the world had professors been given such largess. And never had society reaped such a bountiful harvest. Although the knowledge explosion started slowly, it has accelerated in American universities and colleges at a rate certainly never dreamed of by our founding fathers. Even Jefferson apparently did not foresee what would be produced in college and university activity when he sired the idea of state-supported institutions of higher education.

Perhaps the most important single consequence, however, has been something that is not often recognized. Although universities are publicly justified on the basis of educating the next generation, only about a third of a scholar's time is actually spent in a classroom. The rest of it is spent in finding out what to teach, for it does little good to teach something that is not true or to teach something which is true only under certain circumstances and then be unable to specify those circumstances, or to teach something in such a way that no one can understand it. It is almost ironic to call people teachers who devote more than two-thirds of their time to searching and less than one-third to teaching, yet society does just that because the payoff from this division of labor has been so unprecedented and unexpected.

The still-treasured notions that knowledge is God-given and that scholarship is an individual endeavor have protected the right of faculty to use free or nonassigned time in any way they are inclined. So long as a professor can convince people the time is devoted to academic activity he will never be seriously challenged. This is fine for scholars but it makes administrative auditors simply frantic.

Usually a college professor's contract specifies a fifteen-hour per week teaching assignment. In many of the smaller colleges professors actually teach three classes which meet five hours each per week or five classes which meet three hours each per week or some other combination of two- and four-hour classes. These are the actual number of hours of personal contact with students in an instructional situation for which he can be and is held accountable. Generally, schools which have a history of existence for over seventy-five years have modified this assignment in a variety of ways. Many, for example, allow three hours of credit for student advisement and committee work. This reduces the teaching load to twelve hours. If a professor sponsors doctoral students in their research, he may be granted up to one hour of credit for each student supervised or on whose graduate committee he serves. Obviously, this varies some, but serving on anything from three to nine student doctoral committees may reduce his teaching assignment by one more three-hour class. If he should be elected to a top university committee such as the chairman of the Faculty Senate, or the chairmanship of the University Appeals Board or the Research and Publications Committee, he may be granted a reduction in teaching assignment for that year equal to one three-hour class. In addition, if he should secure a research grant from some outside agency which carries a substantial benefit to the university, he may be granted another reduction in teaching load, probably equivalent to another three-hour class. Because of these adjustments, a college professor of some demonstrated competence may find himself teaching only one or perhaps two classes while still being credited with a fifteen-hour teaching load.

Boards of governance, including all but the least informed members of some church-supported schools or state legislators, recognize the tremendous importance of not only allowing, but actually encouraging college professors to use the majority of their time to pursue knowledge. It has become a standard joke among academics that the former dean of a well-known medical school greeted his fledgling physicians with the admonition: "Half of what you will learn here is not true. Now, if we knew which half we would have a pretty good school," and that this could still apply to any other current field of study. Actually, truth appears to be relative to time, place, and circumstance. Scholarship allows us to be more precise in describing those conditions while we search for new and more useful ways of relating to the information. Those persons who emphasize the teaching function of faculty are simply declaring their own ignorance of the state of the world of knowledge. It is a demonstration of demagoguery and fundamentally an antiintellectual posture which could

Various managers attempt to bring under scrutiny and control the unassigned hours of the scholar's time

ultimately destroy the basis for a civilized world. How much more encouraging to accept Professor J. Glenn Gray's description of education as the "Promise of Wisdom." This allows plenty of room for modesty about what we know and places emphasis on the promise, not the practice.

One of the fascinating continuing dramas for college watchers to follow is the attempt by various managers to bring under scrutiny and control the unassigned hours of the scholar's time, without losing the fruits of those unassigned hours, the eminence of the professor. That is, schools become famous only when their professors become productive scholars and publish the results of their scholarship in professional papers and books. These activities bear no relationship to the classroom responsibilities of the professors, but the professor is responsible to the school only for his teaching-load contract. Thus, the school is famous through its association with what a professor does when he really isn't responsible to them. This gives the school officials an exceedingly tenuous claim to the professor's fame and is a source of no little concern to many of them who would like to put institutional fame on a little solider footing. To rub salt in the wound, those scholarly activities which make a professor a valuable faculty member are also the things which make him valuable to others and allow him to earn various amounts of money for speeches and consulting with businesses, industry, various branches of government, professional organizations, and other universities. Sometimes the money which can be earned by this outside consulting is as much as the university pays him for his full-time job, but most often a professor is quite selective about which requests he accepts so he does not allow his money-making to interfere with his scholarship (a fact which is well-nigh incomprehensible to a nonscholar but seems perfectly logical to the scholar—if for no other reason than that you do not destroy the goose that lays golden eggs).

Various rules have been instituted which have been aimed at circumscribing the nonteaching time of faculty. For example, some administrators have decreed that a faculty member must be in his office at least as many hours each week as he teaches classes. The absurdity of this rule is at least three-fold. First, it assumes that because a professor is in his office that he is working. Since the most important work a professor does goes on between his ears it is obvious that this circumstance is independent of either time or place. Second, those professors who teach the least number of hours are required to spend the least number of hours in their offices. Yet it is those people who are actually most likely to put in the greatest number of effective working hours. The rule thus applies to people who aren't doing much of any consequence anyway. Third, people who teach a good many laboratory-type classes such as music and physical education instructors may be required to spend up to sixty hours per week in their offices. To put it baldly, the regulation only succeeds in keeping people in offices whose presence there is inconsequential in the first place. Fortunately, most institutions which have considered initiating such a rule have abandoned it before they had much chance to suffer chagrin from having done something stupid, publicly.

Other proposed regulations have been more serious and have dealt with copyrights, royalties, patents, consulting fees, and other sources of supplementary income. Nearly every major university has at one time or another gone through the painful process of examining possible regulations to see how they might apply to one or all of these sources of income in a specific university. The most famous was the brouhaha in the 1950s at the University of Chicago during the short presidency of Robert Hutchins, probably because of the strong personalities of both faculty and administration involved. The publicity has since died down, but the same controversy arises in another university in another place at another time, and usually the problem is resolved in much the same way but somehow the word doesn't seem to get around.

Usually the controversy starts with the discovery that

Dr. Smartly found it necessary to prepare supplementary materials to cover areas neglected by the text

Professor Smartly has written a book which is making him rich and that it is required for a course he teaches at the university. This discovery is generally made by a member of the Board of Trustees whose wife's nephew is enrolled in the class. The question of conflict of interest is raised and as the local chapter of the American Association of University Professors charges the Board with interfering with Professor Smartly's academic freedom, a full-scale investigation ensues. The investigation is conducted by the Faculty Welfare Committee which is a subcommittee of the Faculty Senate, with the board represented by the President's office staff and the defense handled by the American Association of University Professors. It is quickly established that the Faculty Constitution states that "Academic freedom is the right of members of the academic community freely to study, discuss, investigate, teach, conduct research, and publish as appropriate to their respective rules and responsibilities." When Professor Smartly testifies, he states that he was assigned to teach the class when he first joined the faculty. At that time they were using a text that was not only horribly boring, it was literally riddled with misstatements and didn't even treat the well-known work of Wisely at Yale and Snorkel of Berkeley. After spending the first year searching for a satisfactory text, Dr. Smartly found it necessary to prepare supplementary materials to cover areas that had been neglected by the text. He also began some investigations of his own, one of which brought in a substantial grant from the Rockefeller Foundation and a subsequent Fulbright scholarship which he used to conduct some investigations at the University of Melbourne while he was on sabbatical leave. It was while he was in Australia that he outlined the actual book and wrote much of the material which he hadn't written before. His proposed text was sent to Holt, Rinehart and Winston, Inc. who accepted the manuscript and the rest is history. It is currently used as a text in a similar course in fifty-seven major universities and he has personal letters of congratulations from both Wisely and

Snorkel, although Snorkel did raise some minor points of criticism. While it is true that one of the departmental secretaries typed parts of the book, those sections were for lecture notes and handouts given to students during class. This is only what any good professor would do as a normal part of his preparation to teach a class. Indeed, the position of the AAUP defense is that Professor Smartly did more than what is normally expected. He really did only what an exceptionally conscientious and able professor would do in preparing materials which would be used to teach a class. The fact that fifty-seven other schools adopted his text only attests to his mastery of the area, but is essentially irrelevant to whether Dr. Smartly owes the school any royalties. In summation, the defense pointed out that all personal expenses for the preparation of the book could be deducted before the university could even begin to claim any share of the royalties and any work done before Dr. Smartly joined the university or was done on weekends, evenings, holidays, or vacations would be credited to Dr. Smartly. Furthermore, on the conflict of interest charge it would be up to the university to prove that the students who bought Smartly's book actually were in his class and were coerced by him. The most telling point is that Professor Smartly would not have fulfilled his academic responsibility had he not worked to improve the course he was assigned to teach. It would be a gross injustice to punish him because his work was so successful that he was also financially rewarded by others in the academic world. As is often the case, the obverse of the situation was not brought out in testimony but was the real clincher. If faculty are not encouraged to pursue their scholarship until it becomes visible, they will never become famous. If they are penalized for becoming famous they will only be forced to try to hide their fame and the university loses. It was not lost on the President and the Board that the grant secured by Dr. Smartly was possible because of his competence, not because of the university prestige. As with members of the faculty, the university ultimately must

Really valuable administrators exert every effort to protect their faculties from the orderly intentions of managers

protect the right and opportunity of faculty to become famous and even rich, if for no other reason than that one does not kill the goose that lays golden eggs.

From all such encounters between scholars and managers an eminently workable principle has evolved. Recognizing that the reputation of both the university and the professor are intimately dependent upon the pursuit of knowledge, wise administrators have accepted the rule of thumb that for each hour of teaching, two hours of preparation and grading are required. A professor with a fifteen-hour load, therefore, probably devotes another thirty hours to preparation. He is held accountable only for his scheduled teaching load because no one would presume to tell a professional how to prepare for his classes, but he is admonished that he may exercise his professional judgment in doing whatever he deems to be appropriate to prepare for his teaching duties provided that he does not abuse the privilege.

The operating principle is that of not abusing the privilege of scheduling one's own time, and like all principles it is vague in the extreme because it is general and not specific. But it works pretty well as a guide, because it applies to many situations, not just one or a few isolated ones. The usual interpretation is that where good intentions are evident and where local customs are observed, it is an operational demonstration that professional judgment can be trusted. When the question of propriety is raised, it is up to the accuser to prove violation of trust. This responsibility tends to have a sobering effect on publicity-seeking critics. The upshot is the recognition that applying accounting procedures to academic activities is counterproductive to scholarly excellence. Really valuable administrators are those who exert every effort to protect their faculties from the orderly intentions of managers whether from within or outside the institution. All others are fundamentally antiintellectual and should be disposed of by whatever means seem most expedient and least time-consuming.

5 *On Being a Teacher*

THERE IS probably no aspect of being a college professor which has come in for more study, comment, and discussion than that of teaching. Nearly every university has some kind of recognition such as the Great Teacher or the Outstanding Professor of the Year Award given to a person who is judged to have excelled in his classroom work. That there are such awards attests to the fact that the administrative leaders of most institutions place a high premium on classroom performance. Indeed, it would be most surprising if they did not in view of the fact that the teaching duties of faculties are really the only ones the administrators have any degree of control over. Faculty also have a considerable stake in classroom performance, for this is nearly always one of the factors considered when questions of tenure, promotion, and salary increases arise.

Over the past twenty years this writer has asked colleagues whether they were good teachers. The answer, despite some evidence to the contrary, has always been in the affirmative. When asked why they thought they were good teachers, nearly every one had a different reason to offer. One said he was good because he was suave, charming, and sophisticated in his lectures. Another was good because his notes were well

The teacher is a manipulator of the learning environment

organized and easy to follow. Another because he was extremely careful about his documentation. Another because he kept his lectures refreshed with reports of his current research. Another because he continually pointed out the relevance of his topic to current happenings. Another because he identified the historical antecedents of present events. Another because he challenged his students to defend their opinions. The list was endless. Of course, you would scarcely expect people who make a living by teaching to either be or consider themselves anything less than accomplished teaching pros, but the incredible number of reasons given has still been just a little mystifying if one wished to know what to do to be a good teacher.

The explanation may lie in the complexity of the teaching task itself and also in the variety of activities which are referred to as though they are all one thing: teaching. It has been contended quite properly that one person does not teach another. A teacher can do little other than set conditions for allowing others to learn. A more eloquent statement of the same thing is that "nobody can't teach nobody nothing." The consequence of this observation attests to the functioning of a teacher as a manipulator of the learning environment. When a person shows a change in behavior, learning is inferred to have occurred. Thus what is usually referred to as teaching involves something done by the teacher, a reaction from the learner, and then information going back to the learner on how successful his response was. Even though this is an oversimplified version of what is meant by teaching, it includes the minimal elements involved. The point, of course, is that if something goes wrong in the process it could be because of the method used, poor teachers, inferior students, impoverished materials, or inadequate facilities, each of which can be pointed to by unsuccessful teachers or students with an excellent probability that at least one significant defect can be found which can be used to explain the failure. Generally if you were to ask students about the quality of class instruction, the evaluation may fall only slightly short of profanity. The typical student solution is to upgrade the faculty by raising the standards, i.e., firing the incompetent teachers. Asking faculty the same question may evoke the same profanity, and the typical faculty solution is to raise standards by restricting enrollment to only qualified students. Face-saving is as advanced an art in academic survival as in oriental diplomacy, and just as trustworthy.

The truth of the matter has been a focus of research attention for some time. Much of the research has concerned itself with faculty performance and characteristics. Such things as appearance, training, experience, field of specialization, style, etc. have all been found to be irrelevant. So also have the students' brightness, sex, out-of-school experience, and major field of study. From an analysis of major studies of teaching effectiveness done by Dr. A. M. Fox and his colleagues, it appears that teachers rated as being effective are prepared for their classes and are good communicators. From the numerous studies of student effectiveness, it appears that good students have well-identified goals and a considerable amount of self-discipline.

It should be obvious that professors who teach the advanced graduate students are dealing with the very best students. No matter what the teacher does, the students will almost always make him look good. This observation is borne out not only from experience, but also from the fact that there is a substantial correlation between teacher rating and course level. That is, teachers of advanced graduate courses get the highest ratings, with correspondingly lower ratings through middle and beginning graduate courses then senior, junior, sophomore, and freshmen courses. Furthermore, higher ratings go to teachers of specialized courses in the major area, and then to teachers of general courses for non-majors. If a professor wants to get the highest possible rating from the least investment, he should teach a highly specialized seminar

Preparation is not a simple matter of having a great deal of information

to a small number of doctoral-level graduate students all of whom are in the same department as the professor. It would do no harm to the ratings if the professor were also on their doctoral committees. Unfortunately, beginning professors do not ordinarily have that opportunity open to them. Instead, they get the lower-division, large-section, general-education courses for non-majors who have vague goals, undemonstrated self-discipline, and often ill-concealed hostility. Every card which could be stacked against getting good ratings is present, including the scheduling of the classes at the least convenient times of day. In this formidable arena, the novice professor who wishes to get good student ratings of his teaching skill cannot afford to leave anything to chance.

Probably one error that has been made in our quest for teaching excellence is the failure to believe those colleagues who said they were good teachers even though each gave a different reason. If they really are good, then it is fruitless to try to describe what a good teacher is because each one is different. Instead we may have better success if we try to identify what it is people do to become well prepared and to learn to communicate, and what conditions facilitate them.

Preparation cannot be a simple matter of having a great deal of information. If such were the case, a computer would be a superb instructor. Not that information is not important, but it is not the fact by itself, but rather the interaction effect. The point at which one fact impinges on another where events that really matter occur. This has been pointed out many times and in many ways, but the importance of this truth to one who wishes to be a good teacher cannot be overemphasized. Proper preparation requires that the instructor not only be in command of accurate information, but also that the information be organized and related to information from other areas. Personal experiences and humorous anecdotes may spice up the presentation, but they are no substitute for solid information. Scholarship is essential to good teaching. By itself, however, it is not enough.

The second attribute of effective teaching is communication. Whether this is in the form of lectures, demonstrations, discussions, dialogues, or group reports is of little consequence. The actual form of a class is usually dictated by size, content, level, intent, and location; so most professors find themselves victims of the class assignment rather than masters anyway. The way in which a class is organized and taught is more often dependent upon those factors than upon the desires or even the conviction of the professor as to the best organizational approach.

Obviously the opportunity for effective communication is greatly increased if the students know almost as much as the professor, if the group is small, if the students are interested in the subject even before they take the class and if the professor considers the students kin (i.e. departmental majors). Once again advanced classes more often fit these criteria and once again beginning professors have a snowball's chance in July of being granted an assignment with these conditions. They are back in the lower-level, large-enrollment, general-education offerings where they must demonstrate survival before they have even a prayer of getting the plusher teaching assignments. Somehow they must develop communication to a fine art if they expect to get even moderately good evaluation ratings from their students.

There are no sure general ways of doing this because each teacher has his own assets to capitalize on and liabilities to cover up. To balance the presentations in favor of the assets requires feedback on your faults and then facing your liabilities honestly. This calls for no small measure of moral courage, but it is well worth enduring the scourging. In this day of electronic gadgetry, the cassette tape recorder is an unobtrusive yet effective method of preserving your classroom performance for future dissection. An even more brutal and effective gadget is the video tape recorder which records your voice, mannerisms, and appearance all at the same time. It is probably wise to submit yourself to the video taping only

Students would be unlikely to believe a phenomenon of instant perfection

after you have done some critical evaluation of your spoken performance. Perfection is generally approached only by degrees. To face the combined impact of voice, mannerisms, and appearance simultaneously may be a little much for mere mortals. Furthermore, students would be unlikely to believe a phenomenon of instant perfection. Therefore, it seems more prudent to strive for improvement in only one dimension at a time. In this way you can demonstrate your competence a little at a time with little danger of losing credibility for being a human being. After you think you have learned to parade your assets judiciously, it may be expedient to ask a trusted colleague to sit in on your class to provide expert evaluation. If you are now pretty good, the word will get around. If you aren't, you will still get credit for trying, and often you will get more approval for trying to learn to be good than for actually being good. Potential in a young faculty member is more highly prized than performance because it provides the department with hope for the future, and hope is what keeps scholars going.

It should be apparent that if feedback on performance is essential for judging effectiveness, then feedback from students is the way you can judge whether they understand your teaching presentations. What you think you have communicated and what the students perceive may be two quite different things. Here the time-honored method of asking the students questions in order to find out what they think they heard or saw has never been superseded. Even this procedure however, can be improved by observing certain practices. Knowing the names of the students so you can call on them individually for example, tends to facilitate communication. If the class is very large, a seating chart which is periodically checked for accuracy will allow you to use names even if you don't know them. This has two serendipitous consequences. First, the students will be astonished that anyone knows them. This results in some feelings of tolerance for some of our less

Never give students options unless you are willing to accept their decisions

endearing qualities, thus increasing the likelihood of the students' developing at least a willingness to listen to what we have to say. Second, since they are labeled with a name which is heard by their fellow students, they are apt to not want to disgrace the name by uttering an ill-considered answer. This often results in their taking the class a little more seriously than those other classes where anonymity prevails. Both attendance and interest tend to be up and the students will often do better than students in other sections on the departmental examinations which are used in multisection courses. These consequences often reflect themselves in student ratings of faculty effectiveness which are higher than they perhaps deserve to be. Since all the cards are stacked against beginning professors getting any kind of positive ratings at all, this is not to be considered inconsequential.

Some faculty have been under the mistaken notion that students should have a voice in deciding what to study in a class. This is nonsense for the reason that, particularly at the lower-division level, the students do not know enough about either the subject or related areas to judge the importance of information impinging on other information. This requires the mature judgment of a scholar. Student input can be valuable in suggesting ways of learning about the subject which are more meaningful to them than others and the methods by which they wish to be evaluated, but not in deciding what is to be studied. The important consideration, of course, is never to give students options unless you are willing to accept their decisions.

This caution extends to another practice which can be put to good use. At the start of each new term, every student should be provided an outline of the purpose of the course, the content to be covered, the method of presentation to be used, the activities to be engaged in, the elements and schedule of evaluation, and the bibliography or knowledge sources which will be employed. Suggestions for changing the

The reputation of the department is paramount

outline can be solicited the first class meeting, carefully recorded, and then honored. If the amended outline is fairly
faithfully followed, important deviations explained before
they occur and the evaluations based on the course outline,
activities, and objectives, the instructor establishes an instant
reputation for fairness. In many academic circles the three *F*s
of friendly, firm, and fair have been presented as the magic
formula for achieving high student ratings. This may be correct, but if it seems possible that not all are mandatory, the
one to be surrendered last should be fairness. Caprice and
favoritism are two practices which wreak havoc in any kind
of institutional setting. In colleges where scholarly integrity
is the *sine qua non* of existence, they can be catastrophic. Friend-
liness may make things pleasant for faculty and students alike,
but it is not necessary to the effective functioning of the department. Likewise, firmness may be an admired quality in
some circumstances, but flexibility probably does more to further departmental and university harmony than an unwilling-
ness to hear dissenting opinions. But for fairness there is no
substitute. Therefore, a faculty member who establishes a
reputation for being fair becomes a treasured departmental
possession, and not solely because the students praise his integrity. The reason goes deeper. First, last, and always, the
reputation of the department is paramount. So long as a
professor contributes to that reputation his behavior will go
a long way toward helping him become a permanent departmental fixture of considerable value.

Thus it appears that teaching well requires that the professor first be a scholar of both depth and breadth, and then that
he pay a great deal of attention to whether his attempts to
communicate with students are successful. If they are not, he
must be serious as he searches for better methods of com-
municating. Here, of course, the much-touted gadgetry of
education should be given a fair chance. Visual aids, audi-
ovisual presentations, slides, transparencies, models, artifacts,

programmed modules, auto-teaching packages, tapes, movies, television, guest experts, and field trips are just a few of the helpers teachers may employ. None of them will be effective unless the student relates to them. Regardless of what teaching techniques are used the truth remains "can't nobody teach nobody nothing." To learn, students must react to the presentation whether that is a person, place, or thing. The successful teacher is apt to be the one who honestly faces the fact that communication is a very personal thing between each instructor and each student. Furthermore, it is possible that one technique of presentation may be very effective with one subject area and completely ineffective in another. Universals simply are myths pursued by naive professors and technology hucksters. To become a good teacher, it appears the professor is going to have to work as hard on his techniques of communication as he does on his preparation. No infallible shortcuts for either have yet been discovered. Perhaps, like the Holy Grail, the reward is in the search, for even though one may never become a particularly good teacher, so long as he keeps trying, he will do little to sully the reputation of the department, and that, after all, is the paramount consideration.

6   *On Doing Research*

IN SPITE of the fact that a great many college faculties have spent much time debating the relative virtues of teaching versus those of doing research, it is difficult to understand why. Of course the disagreement arises over a definition of the function of institutions of higher learning. Those professors who conceive of the university as the place where students learn of the wisdom of the past, generally support the "importance of teaching" point of view. Professors who believe the university to be the primary societal institution for the pursuit of knowledge support the "importance of research" viewpoint. As with all arguments, there are apt to be supports for either position which are quite reasonable and easy to accept by any person except someone who represents the enemy camp. Rather than run the risk of supporting one position over another, it can be reasonably contended that, since research activity is an expected part of the functioning of many college professors, it deserves to be acknowledged and dealt with.

Nearly every handbook of faculty rules and regulations will discuss research in some fashion. It may be treated directly with carefully defined rules governing the use of university facilities, prohibitions against the use of animals except as regulated by the local humane society and against the abuse

Nearly every handbook of faculty rules and regulations will discuss research in some fashion

of human subjects except for volunteers and students who are non-majors. Or it may be treated rather indirectly, as when it is mentioned as one activity to be considered when questions of tenure, promotion, and salary increases arise. Nearly always the references will be so vaguely worded that neither the importance-of-teaching nor the importance-of-research camps will be unduly threatened. The interpretation of this apparent contradiction is relatively straightforward if one remembers that nearly every university regulation is ultimately designed to protect the reputation of the departments. No department can long endure the charge that the faculty cares only about research and that students don't count. Nor can a department survive if it is accused of not having generated a new thought since its inception. Thus the department can interpret the regulations so flexibly that faculty who neglect teaching for research or who never do any original work can both be eliminated. The result of this double-edged regulation is to allow for minimum performance in either area provided performance in the other is good enough to compensate for the weaker area. This has precipitated the dictum "if you can't teach, do good research; and if you can't do research, teach good." The cynical middle ground is that if you cannot do either very well, be sure you do both or else become an administrator where you can do neither and be immune to criticism.

Most institutions expect research activity to take place, so they make provisions for it. Where the publish-or-perish regulations exist, the universities are apt to have fairly elaborate facilitating conditions established. Institutions that do not actively support this tradition may have loose, no, or obstructing rules. Thus opportunities for research vary greatly from one institution to the next and sometimes between departments in the same school. Even when the rules are explicitly stated they are interpreted by people and it is the interpretation, not the rule which counts. Nonetheless, we start with what the rules say and interpret later.

In many schools, faculty regulations state that a given fraction of a professor's assignment is specifically for research. This is generally small for the beginning faculty member and becomes larger as the professor gains stature from his work. The university is always careful not to surrender much time to the control of faculty unless there is near certainty that the reputation of the institution will be enhanced. The obverse, of course, is that if the professor is not or cannot be productive, his time investment will be less damaging to the reputation of the school if it is confined to classroom teaching. The logic of this position seems a trifle thin, but the practicality is obvious: if fame is to be courted, it will be in the research domain or not at all.

Most often, a professor must inform the department chairman about his research activity. This may be anything from a one-line title of the work to a several-page detailed proposal. Usually if the work requires outside funding the elaborate proposal is required. This is considered necessary so the administration can be fully informed concerning any institutional commitments of time, money, facilities, materials, equipment, or personnel. It also serves the purpose of requiring review by competent scholars before the request is sent to granting agencies. This makes it possible to intercept any sloppy, ill-conceived, or otherwise potentially embarrassing proposal before it reaches outside agencies' eyes. Because the agency panels who review grant requests are made up of faculty members from other universities, the reputation of not only a professor, but also a total institution can be made or broken by the review. It isn't so much a matter of whether the request is supported or not. Rather, the quality of the proposal becomes common cocktail-hour gossip, one of the all-time most effective systems for message dissemination. In what often seems to be only a matter of hours, the quality of the proposal is known throughout the entire academic community. Actually there is nothing very mysterious about what

The quality of the research proposal becomes common cocktail-hour gossip

happens. Professor Olds, on the review panel, calls his wife back in University City. She asks how the reviews are going and he mentions that they got a dandy or lousy proposal from Professor Young at Princetown. After he hangs up the phone, Mrs. Olds calls Professor Nice to remind him to substitute for Professor Olds on the Graduate Council meeting tomorrow. Professor Nice asks how things are going and is given the message Olds gave his wife. Next day when the Graduate Council meets, Nice reports he is substituting for Olds who is reviewing proposals for the National Foundation for Research in New York. Somebody asks how it is going and gets the same Olds message given Mrs. Olds and Professor Nice. After the Graduate Council meeting, someone has coffee in the faculty club and the message goes on and on around the campus. Meanwhile, a colleague from the University of Ontario calls someone who was in the faculty club and the reputation of Professor Young and/or Princetown University gets an international flavor. None of this is deliberate, but it does happen, and it happens often enough to be of real consequence to a proposal writer. At least it is a serious enough problem that some schools have their own review panels who look carefully at anything which is going to be sent to a funding agency to be sure it will properly reflect the institutional image before it leaves the campus. Obviously, professors who write good proposals are apt to be well thought of both at home and abroad. It is a condition well worth pursuing.

In an effort to secure somewhat better considerations, some inexperienced professors seek to join with a well-known colleague on joint projects. This is an almost sure quick trip to nowhere. First of all, if it is a project outside the known interest of the senior professor, the rest of the academic world will know that the junior professor did all the work but shared the credit. This establishes him as both insecure and gullible. Second, if the work is in the interest area of the senior professor, it will be assumed that the conceptualization and organization are attributable to him and the junior professor simply assisted in the capacity of a clerk. Within a short time only the junior professor, his wife, and one or two naive graduate students will remember that senior and junior collaborated. Even the senior professor will have forgotten. If the purpose of the collaboration is to provide an apprenticeship opportunity, then joint projects are useful. If they are seen as clever roads to instant fame, the schemer deserves to be disappointed. Scholarship is a solitary pursuit in which there are no shared rewards.

Many schools have rather substantial funds and facilities which are used to support faculty research. For the most part, however, institutional funds are often used as risk capital to support pilot projects in uncertain areas which can then be expanded to generate large grant proposals to major foundations such as Ford and Rockefeller. One scheme in a particular school provided university support for a study. When the study was completed, it was written up as a proposal and submitted to a granting agency. Funds secured to support that proposal were actually used to conduct a second study. Then the first study was written up and submitted as a progress report. In this way, the school was always one study ahead of its requests, thus assuring financial support on an almost continuing basis. Even if a study was a complete fiasco, the support funds of some twenty-five percent of the total cost of the research meant full recovery of funds from only four studies. Furthermore, the department justified adding staff on the basis of research activity, so faculty was pyramided via the sure route of being able to predict grant funds from year to year by being one study ahead of its requests.

The advantage to the university from this procedure is great, but the advantage to the professor is even greater. Since he only submits proposals on work already done, he never comes up with a clunker. Soon the word gets around that he is a winner and is doing lots of exciting things. This is the stuff reputations are made of. Then, when other proposals are sent to the granting agency, they will be expecting good proposals and a halo will immediately attach itself to each document. It is not at all unusual for review committee members to suggest ways of improving a study submitted by someone who has a reputation for doing good work, whereas a nearly identical proposal from an unknown is summarily dismissed. This is not caprice. The granting agency is responsible to its Board of Directors and must demonstrate achievement in the same way any company management must demonstrate profits to its stockholders. Therefore, foundations will tend to support researchers of repute because they can almost be guaranteed results of consequence. Most granting agencies view themselves as investment companies, not as suppliers of risk capital. Furthermore, the more established the foundation, the more stodgy its practices. Fortunately, these practices almost never reach the stage of inflexible scoliosis. Generally about every ten years or so a painful reexamination of priorities occurs and a commitment is made to support new and untried approaches, nearly always in an area of great social concern of at least national scope. Submitting proposals consistent with the current concerns of the funding agency is obviously not just a matter of luck. It pays to monitor the foundation practices, regardless of their stated policies, so new proposal submissions coincide with conscience-examination periods.

In many ways the federal government is similar in operation to private foundations. It has a great deal of money; it uses the same review procedure; the variety of subjects supported is almost limitless; and it is tuned in to current social concerns. It has different constraints, however. Often, for instance, even though appropriations are surrounded by legal directions, the grants are influenced by the current mood of Congress. This is best read in the terminology of speeches made by congressmen who have influential committee assignments. If the committee chairman should identify a "persistent social cancer," any study proposal which attends to "this difficult disease of the body politic; this social cancer," is going to get positive attention. Catch words and phrases make up Washingtonese—the peculiar "in" language of government. Since politicians work so consciously to invent phrases which are memorable and quotable, proof of their success is demonstrated when these phrases become part of the bureaucratic jargon. It is a tricky game to strike the balance between using just the right amount of jargon to demonstrate awareness yet not too much to invite a charge of slobbering. Practiced profitably by experts, the name of the game is grantsmanship. Lest this seem simple, remember the successful grant writer must know the legal constraints, the current social climate, the mood of key congressional figures, and the jargon balance required to present a convincing proposal. It takes a consummate artist to blend these elements into an eye-catching picture. Any faculty member who demonstrates success is apt to be considered a property well worth keeping.

Once the proposal has been funded, the actual mechanics of doing the study can proceed. It is customary in some European institutions for senior professors to plan the research and have the junior staff or research assistants collect the data. Before you decide that this must resemble a research Valhalla, reflect for a moment that very few discoveries of note come out of foreign universities or from cooperative efforts. Furthermore, since many discoveries are accidental and quite outside the scope of the actual research plan, it is obvious that the discoverer needs to be in personal touch with the data source if he is to have any chance at all to identify that happy accident. In other words, while scholarship is dependent upon the available data, the scholar is not. Indeed only he can give meaning to the material. Unless the scholar is superior to his data, he is not a scholar; he is a clerk. The conclusion to be drawn is that there is no easy road to scholarly fame. It is best

Many discoveries are accidental and quite outside the scope of the actual research plan

traveled alone, probably slowly, and with infinite attention to detail. Of course, once fame has been achieved then others can be called upon for assistance. This allows the scholar more time to make speeches (for a modest honorarium) about those discoveries which made him famous and about which he is not modest. By this time, the likelihood of another astonishing accident is so remote that the senior scholar can afford to leave the labors in the hands of lesser lights. Should a "glory hole" be uncovered, his reputation can become even greater if he gives full credit to his associates. Once one is already well known, casting the bread of shared credit on the waters will probably yield about a tenfold return. This could scarcely be considered a poor interest rate, particularly since modesty is being invested and that is not a commodity held dear by most scholars.

Most scholars have a collection of dandy papers, manuscripts, and studies of acceptable quality which were rejected by professional journals as unsuitable for publication. The reasons are myriad and defy logic. One of the problems of doing research on a currently popular subject is the probability that others are doing much the same thing. Submitting a paper to a journal at the same time half a dozen others are received can easily make you a recipient of a "the management regrets" letter. The law of supply and demand is as operable in academia as in economics.

Another common reason for seemingly unreasonable rejection is the failure to relate the paper to anything previously written in the area. The search for knowledge is a parade of efforts by keen minds and curious spirits. Any attempt to enter the parade without acknowledgment of the concept of continuity is apt to be met with no encouragement. If your letter of rejection sarcastically refers to your abysmal ignorance of classical work in the field, you can be sure you committed the sin of insularity.

Provincialism is another frequently unrecognized reason for

The driving force of scholars is eternal optimism

rejection. Often, in the social sciences studies which deal with essentially rural problems tend to evoke a ho-hum reaction when reviewed by academicians from the east. The converse is also true. This is particularly disconcerting when the manuscript is a book which lends itself well to textbook adoption in local universities but is seen by reviewers a thousand miles away as being of remote interest only. To the writer, the problem addressed is real, vital, immediate, and here. Unfortunately the reviewer is the captive of his surroundings just as surely as is the writer. The easy solution is to insist on a friendly neighborhood reviewer. The better solution is to write to the conceptual principle involved since principles have general applicability or, at the very least, to identify where your efforts fit in the knowledge parade. This tends to attach the promise of generality to efforts otherwise pegged as provincial. Whether they are or not is largely irrelevant. Promises frequently carry more weight than they deserve because the driving force for scholars is eternal optimism. Only a fool would scoff at something so powerful.

There is a constant need for critical evaluation of all academic efforts of a research nature. But the acceptability of criticism is based more on the credentials of the critic than on the logic of the arguments. This is not to suggest that researchers are illogical. Rather, a scholar who attacks a popular practice or viewpoint has to first have proved his willingness to be criticized by having published his own work. Thus a perfectly legitimate attack by an unknown person may reap only a letter of rejection, whereas an almost identical reaction from an established scholar not only results in publication, but probably wins an award.

Not all of this can be put down to universal injustice. There is a common bond among the published scholars which transcends petty and sometimes even monumental jealousies. On the surface it appears to be based on the recognition that each has traveled the demanding road of the scholar and is therefore a fellow traveler with all others. This is probably partly true, but is not enough to explain the phenomenon of belong-ingness. Brotherhood is established through enduring common risk, and risk is a corollary of publishing. For every time you publish anything which extends man's knowledge, you invite the meticulous scrutiny of colleagues. If they can find anything questionable in your work, they have the moral obligation to identify it, comment on it, and criticize it. Thus with each publication, a scholar exposes himself to a charge of being either a liar or a fool. It is this risk, from which there is no opportunity to hide, that binds scholar to scholar. The price of membership in this fraternity is to expose your best efforts naked, unprotected, and helpless for all the world to see and criticize. Those who have displayed this kind of cour-age are forever linked to all others. It is not a fellowship of protection, but one of understanding, respect, and commisera-tion. Since the pursuit of knowledge depends upon continued scholarly work and its publication, it is understandable that some courtesies are extended those who have published which are not necessarily offered those who are only pledges and not yet full-fledged members of the fraternity.

While there is no way to eliminate the possibility of being accused of lying or being stupid, there are precautions which can reduce the possibility of the charges being true. In the matter of lying, this is entirely in the control of the researcher. The danger is not so much a matter of deliberately falsifying data. Very few people are deliberately dishonest. Most of us are only a little bit crooked and therein lies the risk. The temptation to ignore information which is not compatible with our stated hypothesis is completely consistent with hu-man nature. This is where the often-heard concern for objec-tivity applies. Objectivity in research is not only nonsense, it is actually counterproductive. Unless a person is thoroughly committed to a point of view, he has trouble generating the enthusiasm to sustain himself through the drudgery of data

There is a temptation to ignore information which is not compatible with our stated hypothesis

gathering. However, once the findings are in, then unless he is completely honest with himself, the tendency to ignore irregular or unexpected findings is just overwhelming. When the work is published, any such oversights will become readily apparent to colleagues who are at least as bright as the researcher and probably a good deal more knowledgeable. It saves a good deal of possible embarrassment if you recognize that being dishonest is just too much work to be worth it. You can't get away with it anyway, so you might as well be virtuous from the outset.

Unfortunately it is more difficult to avoid the charge of being a fool. In this area we are the victims of our own biases and perceptions. In many instances we simply do not see relationships because we are looking at the wrong things. This may not be native stupidity. More likely it reflects our expectations or not being able to see the forest for the trees. Or we may rationalize away findings because they are not exactly what we want to believe. This is not quite the same as dishonesty. Dishonesty is knowing the data is contradictory, stupidity is not recognizing the contradictions.

At present there is no known cure for being a fool. Practically translated, this means you must depend upon other people for salvation. Many professors credit their students as the ones who keep them from making foolish statements. This seems a little overly generous in view of the fact that students generally are unreliable critics. Often students feel they have a great deal to lose if an instructor does not like them. While there may be some punitive professors, there are probably not as many as students would like to believe. Nevertheless there is no doubt a reluctance for students to be as severe in their criticisms as professional colleagues would be, just in case they are dealing with a sensitive ego. Another limiting factor is that students are not as well-informed as professors. This is not necessarily true in individual cases, but it does hold true for the averages. Therefore, the students cannot be as critical as their better-informed professors, because they don't know as much. Furthermore, the ideas presented to students are often verbalized in lectures rather than written in published form. Reactions to orally presented propositions can never be as deliberate as reactions to materials which are read, thought about, and perhaps reread. Those professors who submit their ideas to students may be protecting their personal feelings by consulting courteous critics, but they run the risk of losing the very thing they are seeking — the avoidance of foolish statements published for all the world to see. It is far better to suffer some bruised feelings at the hands of an honest colleague than to be labeled a fool by the larger academic community because we are reluctant to face reality squarely.

There is an additional dividend which accrues to those who submit their work to the critical appraisal of colleagues before publishing, and that is the opportunity to duck responsibility but at a very high level. If you acknowledge the help of Professor Zinger who read and critiqued the manuscript, you can privately always blame him for not eliminating all the errors while publicly appearing to be generous in sharing credit. That way you get the best of all worlds — protection from appearing to be foolish yet someone to blame it on if you don't make it.

7   *On Being Famous*

SEEKING TO become rich and famous is traditionally the American Way. This is no less true for professors, except the order is reversed. It is famous, first, and then rich. Furthermore, since professors are continually on the forefront of their fields of knowledge, the opportunity for achieving fame is extremely good. The chance of acquiring a fortune is considerably less, so it is probably a good thing fame is considered more important.

There are a great many different kinds of fame one can seek in the academic world and there are probably as many different degress of fame as there are kinds. All things considered, the actual degree of fame may not be very important. Not that all degrees are equal. There is a great difference between winning a Nobel Prize and getting an article accepted by a respectable journal, but they are alike in that they both represent the recognition of academic accomplishment, and the recognition of accomplishment is what makes for fame. It is nice to win a Nobel Prize, but it is not necessary. Most professors survive quite well on a considerably lesser degree of fame. It doesn't take much reinforcement to sustain academic effort, just some at frequent intervals will do it. The kind of fame one seeks may be a completely different story from how much, however, for the kind determines how one invests his time.

The academic world provides a built-in system of rewards which provide a small but important measure of fame for the faculty. When a person is hired, he typically is given the academic rank of assistant professor. This title simply means that the person has the minimal training and degrees demanded of university faculty and is presumed qualified to practice the art of college professoring. During the remainder of his college career the professor will be evaluated by a variety of people on a variety of activities, each of which will play a part in his achieving scholastic success.

The first hurdle is that of tenure. Many schools tie tenure and promotion in rank together, but others do not. They are, in fact, separate. Tenure is the contingent right of a faculty member to retain that position granted him until retirement or removal for cause. Practically it means the faculty member's job security cannot be subject to the whim of an administrator or the caprice of the Board of Trustees. The faculty member is free to devote his talents to whatever academic pursuits seem important to him. He is held responsible for using his talents effectively, but not necessarily popularly nor even wisely. Dismissal can be for failure to meet classes, or failure to serve on committees, or failure to do research or publish, but not on whether he teaches, serves, or studies areas approved by other people. Tenure guarantees his scholarly right to self-determination, but it does not protect him from his own incompetence. Proving incompetence is so difficult, however, that the road to tenure is deliberately strewn with obstacles designed to assure that competence has been demonstrated before tenure is offered. Promotions are based on the same criteria as tenure, but they differ in that promotions reoccur while tenure only comes up once. More important, tenure is often voted on and may be denied simply because your colleagues do not like to think of having to work with you for the rest of their academic lives. Promotion is more likely to be independent of popularity, since it is based on accomplishment.

The first hurdle is tenure

It is almost unbelievable that such a vital conceptual principle which came into being to assure that society would not lose the creative genius of its scholars through the caprice, ignorance, or fears of academic administrator-managers could have been inverted in implementation with such apparent ease and so little resistance. Instead of protecting the right of free inquiry of scholars, the tenure process more often may be used to coerce scholars into conventional, noncontroversial, and often trivial academic pursuits. While these procedures assure that the institution will not be embarrassed by the activities of the faculty, they also are not apt to be counted among the worlds' greatest generators of new ideas.

If this condition had come about as a consequence of some dastardly conspiracy, the culprits could be hunted down and shot. Unfortunately it seems to be the result of one of life's little ironies and therefore more difficult to solve. It seems to have occurred largely because tenure is granted early in a professor's career; so early the young professor has not yet achieved much if any measure of fame. Thus the professor has little in the way of substantial accomplishment to prove either to the university or to himself that he is a valuable property well worth protecting with tenure. This makes tenure time an era of uncertainty for everyone, but institutions are better able to capitalize on the opportunity than are faculty. The fact that the supply of potential professors nearly always exceeds demand assures that if a university chooses not to grant tenure to a faculty member, he can be easily replaced. But for the faculty member with few accomplishments as credentials, finding a suitable position after having been denied tenure is no task to dismiss lightly. Thus all the trump cards are held and played by administrators.

Ideally, society would be much better served if the situation were reversed. If a professor could coerce the university administration into providing suitable time, facilities, and materials to support his scholarly efforts the world of academic discovery would be measurably improved. It would be better if, when tenure time arrived, the professor could say, "No thanks. I won't waste my time and talents in a school which values my potential contribution to society so little it will not provide a suitable climate for my growth and development." This could happen if faculty would exercise the option of choosing to accept or reject a tenure offer instead of being so desperately afraid the college will not offer it. Such a happy circumstance seems so remotely possible that it is scarcely worthwhile even hoping for it, so an alternative strategy must be sought. Fortunately there is one.

After a professor has achieved a measure of fame, university administrators often belatedly provide the kind of support which should have been offered much earlier in the professor's career. By this time, the professor can find positions in other universities with relative ease. He is recognized as a valuable property and may even be actively wooed by other schools. Fortunately many succumb to the courtship and move in to take up residence in other quarters. Thus schools which use tenure for coercion tend to lose their really outstanding faculty after awhile. This is not only poetic justice; it is about the only way faculty can strike back at this destructive practice. Unfortunately, quite often boards of trustees and administrators don't recognize what is happening. One mark of second-rate institutions is that they have a record of losing their outstanding faculty to other schools. The only really good avenue open to faculty, therefore, is to pursue fame with passion and then exercise the options which should have been theirs at tenure time. It is, after all, only prudent to circumvent obstacles which cannot be surmounted, and professors need to be considered prudent if nothing else.

Most universities expect the faculty to engage in teaching, research, and service. Therefore the evaluation of faculty performance is largely in those three areas. It is not uncommon that a university will require an annual faculty report form to be filled out which details the professor's accomplishments in each area. Student-filled-out rating forms and sometimes visits by departmental chairman are used to judge teaching effectiveness. In some schools these may be supplemented by descriptions from the professor of those things he has done to make his classes more vital, but this is not necessarily so. In all cases, the professor is expected to present evidence demonstrating that his classroom presence is consistent and his performance acceptable. While the weight accorded this aspect of his work may vary from little to lots, most schools acknowledge a ratio of one-third for teaching, one-third for research, and one-third for service used to provide an accumulated score that can be compared with other professors in determining competence. Obviously if a school uses fifty percent teaching, thirty percent research and twenty percent service, any professor who wants recognition will invest his major efforts in teaching, since that is the area of greatest return. The point is that outstanding performance is required in each area for getting a minimum rating. Conversely, no one can get even a minimal rating unless he is at least acceptable in the teaching area. The university simply cannot afford to risk its reputation at the hands of a drone. If a professor is judged to be not very able as a teacher, he can be tolerated provided his research and/or service functions are outstanding, but if the department perceives that he is giving them a bad reputation because of his teaching, he will never get tenure. Whether we like it or not, professors are first and foremost expected to be teachers.

The annual report form will also provide space to list any publications, whether they are books, articles, or monographs. The critical point is not so much whether someone has published — because everyone is expected to — but who has published his stuff. For articles, journals sponsored by professional societies have the highest prestige, then journals published by college and university research bureaus, and last,

The critical point is who publishes your stuff

commercial companies. The order is not the same for books. Here the university presses are most prestigious, then the large commercial firms, and finally, the do-it-yourself firms who require you to guarantee the sales of a certain number of copies before you share in the royalties. The prestige of the publisher is dependent upon the difficulty of getting manuscripts accepted. Most university presses look at the scholarly value of the books since the reviews are done by professors of some note. The commercial companies also have professors review the manuscripts, but the final decision is on merit tempered by probable sales with the nod going to the sales end. Scholarly merit, therefore, tends to be of lesser importance.

Room is also provided on the report form for listing research projects either completed or in progress and sources from which support funds have been obtained. Of principle importance is whether the research is funded, by whom, and for how much. Again, funding is important, but brownie points accrue more depending upon where the funds come from than simply how much they are. Universities also apparently would rather be famous than rich. In any event, they prize funding from prestigious foundations more highly than from governmental sources, even when they get less money from the foundations. However, they do not always consider funding from outside agencies of greater importance than funds secured from university research funds. This apparent paradox is easily understood when you recall that fame is held dearer than riches by the university administration as well as by scholars. Since the university funds are considered risk capital, they are more apt to be granted to support a far-out idea than a more conventional study, simply because the unique idea may open up a whole new field for study and the university can claim motherhood. Even if the effort is a fiasco, university administrators can tell and retell the story of Professor Blankly's folly and with a judicious embellishment or two make the university look good even in defeat. Parkinson's principles of gamesmanship are as valid for institutions as for persons.

The services engaged in by college professors are nearly as many and varied as there are professors. Some services command rather substantial fees, while many (or perhaps most) do not. The apparent paradox is that quite often the free services may be more highly regarded by university officials than those services which are paid. To add to the complication, even among those services for which fees may be expected, there is often no relationship between the amount of money earned and the apparent worth of the service.

Consultation is one of the more commonly pursued activities of professors. The fact that nearly any faculty member will have the opportunity to share his expertise with others simply underscores the assertion made earlier that professors are apt to know a great deal about their fields. The importance of those who demand the services and the kind of service requested are key factors in judging the worth of the consultation. Being selected as a consultant/expert for any one of the federal departments is a great recognition of expertise, but not as high as being a consultant for special projects. Of nearly equal importance is an appointment to a national advisory council of some kind. These appointments are a clear recognition of expertness, but they are made by the current President and even though competence is a criteria in selection, it is tempered by political considerations. Given equally qualified people, the one with a political persuasion compatible with the party in power will be tapped. This is all right, because the chances are that the next vacancy to be filled will occur when there has been a party change, so the politics even out after a while. The selection of special consultant is made by people who are chiefs of various kinds in the Washington bureaus and divisions. Since these people are usually career civil servants with excellent professional credentials of their

own, you must be outstanding to get their approval. Therefore, the prestige connected with that kind of appointment far
outweighs presidential notice. A somewhat more often over-
looked difference also has a profound effect on the importance
of consulting for the federal government. Generally, advisory
committees are made up of a large group of people; perhaps
as many as twenty-one in all. Although the committee may
have enormous influence, each person typically has very little.
Furthermore, the committees control policy which has a long-
range effect on practice, so their influence is seen as remote.
Review panels made up of consultant/experts implement the
policies of the advisory committees by funding programs.
These are small committees of perhaps five to nine members.
The influence of one person is therefore greater and more
immediate. The special consultant often works alone or with
only two or three others and generally on projects not specifically covered by policy or regulations. His influence is therefore in both setting precedent and recommending funding, so
he may exert great influence on both long-term and immediate
practices. Fees proffered by federal agencies are so miniscule
as to border on penury. Nevertheless, the distinction of being
selected for any federal consulting is so great there is never
a shortage of candidates. Interestingly enough international
consultation is generally viewed as not particularly important.
There are perhaps many reasons for this, but among the more
identifiable is the feeling that some foreign governments may
not be as concerned about social betterment for those who
really need it as they are for the political advantages of giving
the appearance of concern. In the economic, industrial, and
defense arena there is probably some reluctance to share secrets or give any edge to other countries which could someday
use those bits of knowhow to our disadvantage. Professors are
certainly no less and could be somewhat more reluctant than
any other group of people to be exploited. To have been
duped, or used, or had, goes a long way toward drying up the

well of human compassion. Somehow this seems to happen more often in encounters with foreign governments than it does with our own. Or maybe it's just more noticeable when done by someone who is not a member of the family. In any case, it is considered better to be a national than an international consultant.

State governments are quite often miniatures of the federal government, with some rather noteable exceptions. The advisory committees are the most prestigious because they typically are formed to determine just how federal funds should be spent. The wisdom which attends this task could well determine the amount of money forthcoming for future ventures of a similar nature. Therefore, since great power is wielded by the committees, great importance is attached to committee assignments. Conversely, consultation with departments of state government is not accorded much account. This difference between state and federal consulting is readily understood in light of state functions. For the most part, state legislators are apt to be considerably more enduring than elected officers. Furthermore, the political kingmakers are those people who can influence state regulations and laws and therefore are likely to be found firmly entrenched in the legislature. The role of the governor tends to become ceremonial and persuasive rather than that of an executive with much enduring power. State departments, therefore, become quite sensitive to the wishes of the legislators. As such, they become immersed in regulatory functions or in the monitoring the compliance of agencies with state laws. Working with state departments often means the professor is called upon to suggest better management techniques rather than better programs since the programs are determined by state legislation. Unless the professor's area is public administration, he ordinarily doesn't find this overwhelmingly creative or rewarding. Since state governments often pay even less for consulting than the federal government, the skepticism about whether your contribution of time and effort will be suitably rewarded is neatly confirmed.

Every professional specialty has its own organization with its own journals. To survive, the organization must have leaders and an annual convention. Although considerable cynicism surrounds the purposes of the organizations and the need for conventions, they are a fact of academic life and are important and fragile enough to demand protection. The organizations and conventions do perform necessary services for universities and their faculties. Among the more important is that of providing an outlet for articles either at conventions or in the journals. Although the published paper is more to be desired than the paper delivered at a convention, both are life's blood to the academic body of knowledge, and neither would be possible without a living, breathing, professional organization to sponsor them. For this reason, if for no other, services to the professional associations are highly prized by university administrators and rewarded accordingly. Although national offices are considered of greatest worth, officials of regional, state, and local chapters are given considerable credit. While not every local officer will grow up to be national president, there is always that possibility, and no institution with decent maternal instincts will take a chance that it will be somebody else's favorite son. Obviously the more faculty a university has holding various offices, the better the odds of producing a winner.

In addition to service to the professions, college professors are probably more socially conscious than many other citizens and are quite likely to be called upon to perform in the civil service arena. Not a few former professors have also been congressmen, senators, supreme court justices, and even presidents of the United States. Even more have been on school boards or city councils or have been mayors, and a great number have been actively involved in civic clubs or church activities. Whether these latter two should be considered of significant service to the community is not really a matter for debate. Communities would be the poorer if either institution were to disappear, so civic club activities and church work are both eligible for inclusion in the annual faculty activity form. It should be cautioned however, that unless the activities bring a great deal of favorable publicity to the university, they will not generate much credit toward either tenure or promotion. It may be nice to be able to point to church membership of faculty when the university is accused of being ungodly, but since that charge arises less often with each passing decade, the fact of membership is rapidly losing its former punch. Civic club membership is about equally unimportant except for small towns in the midwest. Neither, therefore, is apt to be able to compensate for deficiency in the more important areas of research and teaching.

Of considerably more weight are faculty services to the university itself. Even though universities appear to differ, there is a remarkable sameness in their governance organization. Generally at the top is the University Senate, made up of elected faculty proportionally representing the various colleges, schools, and departments. The senate deals with all the functions which affect the entire university: calendar, personnel policies, programs, requirements, leaves of absence, general budgets, grading systems, student activities, and university crises. The list is apparently endless but becomes manageable because some problems are disposed of each year (despite beliefs to the contrary), and these become operational policy which need only periodic review. Also many areas of concern are assigned to standing committees, such as Faculty Welfare, Academic Policy, Graduate Council, Research and Publications, Curriculum, Student Personnel, Activities Coordination, Athletic Control and various temporary committees formed to deal with specific but short term problems. Reports and recommendation from these committees to the senate make it possible for the senate to keep up with the needed changes in university policy in a surprisingly efficient manner. Contrary to apparent logic, the prestige accorded membership of these committees is not based on the position of the committee in the governance order. Instead it is related to the perceived effect the committee has on the work conditions of faculty. In many universities, funds to support research and released time to devote to research are allocated by the Research and Publications Committee. In publish-or-perish institutions, membership on this committee is the top assignment and the chairmanship of the committee is of greater importance than any academic titled position, including President of the university. In other institutions where research is not highly rewarded or conversely where lack of research activity is not severely punished, various ad hoc committees appointed by the president or the senate to study curricular reform or administrative reorganization or something equally threatening to the status quo would be considered to carry great recognition to the appointees. Generally speaking, committees of an all-university nature have the greatest prestige, then all-college, then school, and finally departmental committees have the least — except this ordering does not apply to all-university activities or student problems. The Board of Athletic Control, for example, is ordinarily considered unworthy of the concern of faculty, except for someone who wants free passes to the athletic events. For serving on the board he gets the passes, but virtually no credit toward rank, pay, or tenure. The committee for Activity Coordination which sponsors lectures, appearances, art films, and homecoming is in the same league as the Board of Athletic Control. They are joined in the prestige cellar by any committees designed to further student welfare. Despite the fact that these are all-university committees with noble purposes, they have almost no effect on the operation of the departments so they are tolerated but ignored. It isn't that they are discriminated against; rather they are just treated as though they don't exist.

Select a committee assignment which has the power to frighten your colleagues

That kind of neglect does little to make the professors on the committees feel vital and appreciated. The moral, of course, is that any faculty member who seeks recognition through service had better select a committee assignment which has the power to frighten his colleagues. Innocuous committees that do good things certainly do not meet this requirement.

Every professor can go through the stations of the institution by performing in the manner expected. Typically, an assistant professor will be promoted to associate professor if during the five years or so he holds assistant rank he gathers some evidence to demonstrate he was an effective if not outstanding teacher, that he carried on research of his own, some of which was funded by outside agencies, and that his work resulted in publications of a scholarly nature. In addition he may have acted as a consultant, conducted workshops or clinics, served on professional boards, taken an active part in the professional association of his special field, and been on his fair share of the committees which proliferate throughout the university, college, school, and department. It would also help if he performed some service important to the community he lived in. From these activities promotion will be forthcoming provided his appearance, behavior, beliefs, manners, and morals are not subjects of too much embarrassment to the institution. Although this list of expected accomplishments may appear formidable, it should be remembered that not all are required. Even though they are cumulated, for the most part, compensation is the rule rather than the exception. No one is expected to be a paragon of all virtue—just some.

The difference between an associate professor and a full professor is another five years or so of experience and several light-years in performance. Whereas an assistant professor needs to establish a record of accomplishment in perhaps three or four of the many activities for which credit is given, the person who wants to be promoted to full professor will need to demonstrate competence in twice as many. The time-worn

Few faculty seem to want to become famous as teachers

quip that the difference between an assistant and associate is a couple of articles but the difference between an associate and a full professor is a book, does have an element of truth. Fortunately, it remains a quip rather than a principle. It is still possible for professors to gain promotions without being published. Since this undoubtedly results in the publication of fewer books that would probably appear if publication were an inflexible requirement for promotion, we should treasure the exceptions. We are surrounded with quite enough dross in printed form which is gratuitously presented. It is not necessary to legislate that there shall be more.

Curiously enough, even though faculty have to do about the same things to be promoted as other faculty, there is still some free choice of the arena within which professors can seek their fame. Few faculty, for instance, seem to want to become famous as teachers. Even though the annual Great Teacher Award is rather substantial (typically a thousand or more tax-free dollars) it is generally not a very coveted kind of recognition. Not that it is ever refused by the recipient, it is simply not sought. There are probably many reasons why this is true, but among the more important is that all of us prefer recognition by our peers to recognition from our inferiors, and the selection is made by students, alumni, and often some administrative head rather than by faculty; and they are all considered inferior judges. Another reason is that selection is based on opinion, and it is considerably more flattering to have some kind of objective data available to point to for validation than to have to accept unsubstantiated opinion. Somehow it is easier to believe people when it is not necessary to trust them completely. Still a third reason is that teachers exert their influence only on the students who are in their classes, while written articles and books can reach an infinite number of people. But the principle reason may be that teaching has only a passing influence on people; it lasts only so long as the teacher teaches, but scholarly ideas live long after their discoverers are dead and gone. Somehow foregoing the temporary fame derived from good teaching seems a bargain in exchange for the chance of academic immortality.

Of greater importance is the kind of fame one seeks. Essentially, the decision is to seek fame either in the university or outside. This decision divides people into those who are parochial versus those who are catholic, provincial versus cosmopolitan, local versus universal. The dividing line is the city limits, for the locals have little or no stature beyond the city limits while the cosmopolitans may have worldwide fame which seldom penetrates inside the city limits. The chief distinction, however, is more fundamental than mere geography. All fame is derived from visibility. Therefore, local fame is attached to local visibility and the most noticeable faculty in a university are people who have titles. Generally speaking, college presidents, vice-presidents, provosts, deans, directors, and chairmen can achieve local fame without any discernible accomplishments. Faculty who become actively involved in running the university become locally famous within an extremely short period of time and with a minimal record of achievement. Membership on committees provides the necessary visibility and the minutes of the committee meetings provide incontrovertible evidence of nonaccomplishment. The price of this instant notice is apt to be instant oblivion, for when the professor is no longer on committees or head of an administrative unit he is easily forgotten, primarily because he has contributed nothing lasting with which he can be identified. Nearly everything that is done is given committee credit which denies credit to any one person. On the other hand, lack of productivity can be camouflaged by adroit buck passing, thus protecting both the guilty and the innocent. The real winner is probably the rest of the university, for if committees were able to implement all their proposals, it is more than likely that the university would be reduced to a shambles. It is well to remember that a camel has been defined as a horse put together by a committee.

Cosmopolitan fame is considerably longer in coming because it is arrived at through the medium of published professional work. Counting preparation time, publication lag, and appraisal of quality by colleagues, anyone who does anything of note in less than two years is lucky. Furthermore, fame is made up of accumulated work so unless the work is of unusual character, some eight or ten years may pass before much of a reputation is established. Once some recognition is achieved, however, it is a long time dying. It is not at all unusual for a professor to be asked to make speeches about some pioneering work he did twenty years after he lost interest in it and turned his attention to more exciting things. Of course the academic community has only his published works to clue them into the work activities, and often they do not pay much attention to how old the publications actually are. Furthermore, if his work becomes the basis for a book, it may have taken five years to do the research, two years to write the book, two years to get it published, and two years for the book to be very widely distributed. Thus ten or eleven years will have passed before recognition is achieved. Interestingly enough, the things which made the professor famous also make the university famous. Thus the university is able to trade on the reputation of a scholar long after his work has terminated. This accounts for a good many of the disappointments of students who attend a university because of the exciting work going on there only to find the volcano is extinct. Referred to as dinosaur graveyards, these are more often the rule than the exception. The most exciting time in a department is during the period just before it becomes famous. By the time fame has been achieved the excitement of discovery is gone. Although it is impossible to accurately predict which people are going to become famous before they do and thus select a department which is in its ascendance, one system can be used with better-than-average chance of success, and that is selecting a department which has a great scholar as a chairman. He will have both local and cosmopolitan fame,

Nothing helps scholarship so much as being left alone

avoiding the usual dichotomy. He will have gone through all the trials and tribulations involved in achieving recognition for his scholarship and he will be thoroughly conversant with the obligations of administering a department so others will be able to do their own work. More important, he will at least have a chance to understand the price one must pay for each kind of success, so he will be able to distinguish between the superficial and the real. Being a good scholar is no guarantee of being a good administrator, but there is a chance that his loyalty will be to the academic rather than managerial values. At least he will probably know the difference between them, and that is generally more than can be expected from the average administrator. But there is an even more compelling reason to choose the scholar-administrator and that is that if he continues his scholarship he will be so busy he won't have time to bother you much and probably nothing helps scholarship so much as being left alone. It is a condition well worth seeking if you would wish to pursue cosmopolitan fame.

8 *On Coping*

WHATEVER MAY be the academic rank, title, or degree of fame of a professor, each has in common with every other professor the mundane but demanding problem of getting through each day. Furthermore, even allowing for enormous individual differences in location, school size, and special area, the typical problems faced by professors are apt to be not radically different from those faced by their colleagues. The search for a solution to these persisting problems follows a simple principle called coping. This principle states that whatever you do, it will turn out wrong, so you need to find some strategy which will minimize the unfortunate consequences of any action taken.

Many of the problems revolve around the teaching assignment of faculty. Regardless of how a class is organized, the instructor is expected to have used some method to evaluate student performance and this evaluation has to be translated into some hierarchy ranging from high to low. Evaluation schemes are as old and as varied as teaching itself and, uniformly, each is unsatisfactory. They form a scale which is based on the degree to which students have a voice in the evaluation process. A professor who uses paper-and-pencil tests, either multiple choice or essay, would rate very low on

The principle of coping states that whatever you do, it will turn out wrong

the dimension. Even contract grading, by which student has to complete a certain number of projects to earn points toward his grade, still allows very little room for student input. Courses in which students rate the performance of other students score high in student participation, and those in which students assign their own grades are among the highest. Needless to say, it does not take a professor very long to find out that his system of evaluating students becomes in turn the system by which he is evaluated by students. Professors who assign grades with little student involvement are generally considered conservative, inflexible, Republican, square, and old. On the other hand, faculty who use a good deal of student input are usually considered young, naive, pseudoliberal, untrustworthy, not very knowledgeable, and on the make for whatever is available. It takes a consummate artist to devise a grading system with the right balance of student and professor participation so he becomes characterized as knowledgeable, young in spirit, flexible, trustworthy, and available rather than on the make — an important distinction. Like all the principles presented in this section, the principle just articulated does not hold in specific areas. In the social sciences, political economics, minority studies, and educational psychology, student involvement is a way of life. In history, mathematics, the sciences, engineering, agriculture, and home economics it is not. The difficulty involved in devising a grading scheme is that of striking a balance between being considered too strict or too lenient in grade assignments. If you use a relative system, then ten to fifteen percent will earn *A*s, twenty-five to thirty percent *B*s, forty to fifty percent *C*s, and fifteen to thirty-five percent *D*s or *F*s, regardless of their absolute performance. On the other hand, if you use an absolute scale such as so many points for an *A,* fewer for a *B,* etc., theoretically it is possible for everyone to get *A*s and you can get an uneven distribution of grades. Thus, the dilemma is that whichever choice is made, it is a bad choice. The moral, of course, is to

Professors who assign grades with little student involvement are generally considered conservative, inflexible, Republican, square, and old

select whatever grading system is least in line with what your colleagues use. That way, you emerge as creative, and that is a characteristic highly prized by students and faculty alike.

In the course of daily routine, every professor must face the task of advising students. Schools differ considerably in their management of this function, generally in relation to size and source of funding. State supported universities can better afford to pay scant attention to the needs and wishes for personal attention from students since individual taxpayers have virtually no influence on legislative support for these institutions. Humane treatment brings few rewards while callousness costs little. Private schools depend heavily on alumni support, so they tend to be studious in their advisement concerns. The reasons for this are many, but two are most important. First, the advisee could be a son or daughter of a generous alum (because of the peculiarities of divorce, remarriage, and commune customs, surnames have ceased to be a reliable indicator of parentage). It would never do to run the risk of not paying proper attention to the problems of a youngster supported by a potentially openable wallet. Second, the students themselves tend to grow up to be affluent rather than poor. Thus, the long-range interests of the institution demand careful immediate attention to student needs in case they survive the hazards of life and grow up to be affluent.

Advisement, of course, takes many forms, so it is probably both unwise and perhaps impossible to generalize about all aspects, but academic advisement is probably more alike from school to school than other kinds. Typical academic advisement deals with selecting the proper courses in the proper order to assure meeting the university requirements for graduation. There is nothing very mysterious about this process since it's carefully explained in the most precise words possible in the current university catalog. As usual, the hooker is that the program rests on the assumption that each course needed will be offered at a convenient time of day and at an appropriate time of the year to meet the scheduling needs of students. This almost never happens. For one thing, courses are scheduled to provide nearly the same number of courses at 8:00 A.M. as are offered at 9:00 A.M., etc. throughout the day so the maximum use of each classroom in each building is assured. Each department, therefore, distributes its classes throughout the day in such a way that each professor can teach his full load without having all his classes bunched together in the same hour. Thus the classes in a given department are scheduled with virtually no concern over whether they conflict with required courses from other departments. The result is that they nearly always do. Or if they do not conflict in any given quarter or semester, they most probably will in the next one as adjustments are made in the schedule to accommodate program improvement or the fact that Professor Claude is on sabbatical leave and his courses are being parceled out to other members of the staff. Since conflicts are the rule, not the exception, the really prized advisor is the one who is able to suggest course alternatives for those which are scheduled at the same time. Unfortunately, the reward for this creativity is that more and more students seek your expert guidance. The consequence of this condition is that the better you are as an advisor, the greater the demand for your services and the less your opportunity to be a productive scholar, from whence raises in salary and rank emanate. The solution to this apparent dilemma is the simple application of the principle of coping—the principle which emanates from the probability that no matter what you do, it turns out wrong. If you are helpful to students, they will usurp all your time. On the other hand, if you do not help them you will soon get the reputation of being uninterested in student problems or incompetent to solve them. Whether either charge is correct is irrelevant. The important concern is how to handle the problem with a minimum of difficulty. Some professors develop a defensive coloration characterized as concerned bewilderment. They act

The better you are as an advisor, the greater the demand for your services

very interested in the students, but are careful to never let anyone know that they understand the system. Thus, they make a practice of always asking someone else—a secretary, another faculty member, or other students—for answers to advisees' questions. Before long, the students believe that the professor doesn't really know very much about advisement, so they come to see him only for a signature or something equally unimportant. The real problems they take to others who have established reputations for being knowledgeable and helpful. With this system, the professor preserves the illusion among students that he really cares about them, but he successfully gets them to leave him alone because they don't think he can help them. It is not easy to achieve the best of both worlds, but with effort it can be done.

One apparent fringe benefit of being a college professor is being surrounded by probably the most attractive group of people in the country. College students are more pleasant, bright, well-informed, well-mannered, aware, interesting, and good-looking than nearly any comparable group of young people one might find. Precisely because of these characteristics they are a delight to be with and there is a grave temptation for a professor to learn to enjoy their company more than that of his peers. The rewards from joining with students in various activities looms as one of the most insidious influences in academia. First, there are an almost endless number of opportunities for participation, so it is nearly impossible not to find some area in which one has an abiding interest. Thus, it is easy to convince oneself that the concern is for activity, not the company. Second, the activity is nearly always one of obvious significance which does good things for someone. Thus, there is the added reward which comes from feeling you are making a contribution to building a better world and the possibility of accumulating virtue while having fun.

The difficulties which accompany yielding to these arguments are many, but there are two important ones. First, since

Becoming just one of the bunch

you are somewhat older than the students, have more educational degrees, probably have more experience than they, and hold a position in the university which carries a title, you are apt to be treated with some noticeable reserve, if not deference. If you relish the role, you soon become the all wise guru of the Peace on Earth Club or whatever else it is you belong to. This role tends to alienate you even more as time goes on and soon you become a kind of grand old man — tolerated and joked about, but not really taken very seriously. Given this condition, your effectiveness decreases in direct proportion to the amount of deference shown. The converse of this is that of being a buddy. It starts with the announcement, "my friends call me Horatio." Next, the faculty participant in student activities finds it necessary to laud and support student suggestions which are patently idiotic, just to demonstrate respect for their opinions. After a considerable amount of this kind of self-debasement, the students may indeed call you Horatio and drop the deference treatment, acting like you are an equal rather than a superior. When you become just one of the bunch, you have achieved your objective. Unfortunately, colleges are specifically designed to help people grow intellectually. After a suitable demonstration of this growth, students are ceremoniously escorted out the door via the mechanism of graduation. Faculty, however, are not. The students take their growth with them, but faculty must keep theirs in the institution. Thus, the change which has taken place in the faculty member as a result of his participation with students in these activities cannot be shed when a new group of students enter. The new bunch may call you Horatio, but there is every certainty that you will not be able to resist offering that, "We tried that idea last year or two years ago or twenty-five years ago with rather disastrous results." The second that utterance occurs, you become Mr. Guru and your entire "one of the bunch" strategy collapses. The point is that whichever role you adopt, the consequences are destined to become untenable.

A second major problem associated with student activities is one of return on your time investment. Students tend to take their work and themselves much more seriously than either warrants. Faculty generally exhibit a similar character defect. Thus, the student activity, whatever it is, soon begins to claim an increasing amount of time and energy from the participants. As is the case with most activities, the reward is in the doing, not the done. It is extremely difficult to identify concrete changes of any lasting quality which have resulted from student activities. This is acceptable for students, but faculty need to be associated with accomplishment, not just moving around and talking. When raises, tenure, or promotion are considered, they pivot on concrete products which can be pointed to, counted, weighed, collected, and displayed. Activity, no matter how frenetic, fails to meet these criteria. Unless the return on the time investment provides a better yield than having fun and keeping busy, you are well advised to avoid such entanglements. This is not to suggest that the activities are not worthwhile; rather it is to aid you in establishing professional priorities. These activities are named *student* activities because they are for students. This should serve as a warning to professors: be sure you read the label before you buy the product.

Closely associated with student activities are student affairs. These are inevitable on any campus precisely because faculty and students are drawn from larger pools of humans divided approximately equally into men and women. Hormonal activity being what it is, the sexes seek each other out at every possible opportunity. Once again, whatever a college professor chooses to do about sex with students, he makes a bad choice.

Contrary to popular opinion, most opportunities for alliances do not come about when a student offers sexual favors in exchange for a passing grade in a class or when a professor offers a similar rate of exchange. Such a transaction smacks of professionalism, and no pro worthy of the title would offer her wares that inexpensively. Should such an offer be made at all, it would have to be considered either the result of lack of knowledge of current exchange rates, or a true pricing of the actual worth of the service. Neither inspires much confidence in the buyer. One should always be skeptical of apparent bargains when dealing with amateurs.

Most of the time, dalliance follows on the heels of some chance encounter among people who have had some previous, but probably superficial, contact. A professor who is unable to find a table to sit at for morning coffee, spots an empty chair by a former student from one of his classes. A student finds herself sitting next to one of her former teachers at a university lecture or concert or movie. A professor visits a local tavern on Friday afternoon and discovers a group of students celebrating T.G.I.F. (thank God it's Friday), more popularly known as F.A.C. or Friday Afternoon Club. (Why it should be called a club remains one of academia's deep mysteries. It is unorganized, has no membership, no dues, and no club-rooms. Nevertheless, when students and/or faculty decide to visit a local pub to have a drink on Friday afternoon after all their classes are over, it is known as F.A.C.ing. It is a proud and honorable tradition tracing back at least to the famous universities of Heidelburg and Oxford in the 1200s and 1300s and probably back to the early Greeks. Throughout the centuries, alcohol and academias have always been compatible.) From the chance encounter, a kindled interest can quickly be fanned into flame. Probably what used to be the most serious obstacle was the lack of time and place, but with the preponderance of students now living in apartments rather than dormitories, privacy problems presently are not as formidable. Of greater concern is the aftermath. For some reason or other, young people typically do not recognize incompetence in bed any better than they recognize incompetence in the classroom. Just as no one can expect to become a good student without

Young people don't recognize incompetence in bed any better than they recognize it in the classroom

dedication, devotion, and persistence, one cannot become an accomplished sex partner without equal parts of that prescription. In addition, any athlete knows that practice without good coaching only leads to the perfection of improper moves. While breeding may be instinctive, sex is not. Properly cultivated, it must emerge as one of civilized man's finest accomplishments. Without nurturing, it becomes boring—witness the current divorce statistics or the animation of the crowds in porno movies. The main difficulty with casual sex is that it is casual. There is neither the time nor the commitment to develop a relationship which can be instrumented like a finely trained orchestra. This is nobody's fault; it is just the natural consequence of any spontaneous performance. On the other hand, should the professor and student take the affair seriously enough to attend to the nuances of the other partner's moods and behaviors, then the whole thing takes on an air of permanence. Soon subtle demands are extended which imply, if not explicitly state, the duty to recognize things like birthdays and other ceremonial days with special observances. That is, the relationship goes far beyond the bounds of a nice sex relationship and begins to control other aspects of living which have nothing to do with sex. What may have started out as a manageable affair soon becomes a managing one in which virtually every aspect of your life is involved. The price becomes exorbitant, particularly if you, also, have a home, wife and family to maintain. Unfortunately, no very good solution to this dilemma seems available. If either casual sex or committed sex are bad choices, no hanky panky seems almost as bad an alternative. But, as in all coping behavior, sex is another area in which the least bad alternative wins.

The coping process also applies to committee work. Of all the institutional universals, committees are probably the most permanent. So pervasive is the committee system that it seems impossible to imagine a university, college, school, or department without committees. Nearly every faculty regulations

In academia, it is considered more important to talk about a problem than to do something about it

handbook devotes more space to the descriptions of committee structure and functions than to any other single subject. Curiously enough, the prestige of a committee is directly related to the size of the body politic represented. All-university committees are the most prestigious, with all college, school, and department committees following in descending order of prestige. However, the greater the prestige of the committee, and the more permanent the committee, the more likely it is to be useless. That is, committees which are formed to find a solution to a specific problem are apt to be small, made up of people who are judged to have the capability of finding a solution, and very nearly guaranteed to have their proposed solution accepted by their constituents. Since there is then no further need for the committee, it self-destructs. Standing committees on the other hand, are formed to formulate policy statements which deal with insoluable or reoccurring problems. Because of that, they never accomplish anything tangible. In academia, it is apparently considered more important to talk about a problem than to do something about it. For this reason, people selected to these committees are elected and tend to be those who can effect a compromise solution in the form of statements of principle which really don't solve problems, merely specify what the solution should or should not do. To qualify for the standing committees, however, many universities require that faculty must have earned tenure and, therefore, must have been on the staff for several years. More critically, the professor must have earned a reputation for being willing and able to listen to other people's viewpoints and to debate, with courtesy and tact, the merits of each presented position. Most important, he must have demonstrated an ability to support the position that discussion about a problem is of higher priority than eliminating the problem. If you serve on the small, temporary, departmental committees, you will not be wasting your time, but you don't get much credit for it either. On the other hand, if

you earn the right to serve on the more prestigious committees, you can be virtually assured that your time investment
will yield almost nothing in the nature of tangible accomplishment. Furthermore, the probability is quite high that for the
high-prestige committees, a delay of from ten to fifteen minutes in starting the meetings will occur each meeting because
a key member will be late because he has been held over in
another preceding meeting of a committee of equal or greater
stature. If you attend the meeting on time, this will guarantee
a waste of an average 12½ minutes per meeting or 450 minutes per academic year. This amounts to 7½ hours or one
full day per prestigious committee.

There is probably no very good way to cope with this problem, but again one need not be a helpless victim of the system.
Since you can be absolutely certain that someone else is going
to be late for each meeting, you can time your activities so you
arrive exactly ten minutes late. This assures that you will be
on hand when or before the chronic late arriver gets there so
you will not be blamed for holding up the meeting. Most
salutory, you will be getting ten minutes per meeting to use
as you see fit. While this does not yield quite one day per year
of free time, it does give you a full six hours gratis and that
is long enough to crank out another publication if you work
diligently.

An even more effective strategy was suggested by Ogden
R. Lindsley. Since there are too many kinds of retribution dealt
to people who appear to reject the obligations of the committee system, it is not worth the punishment to ignore or refuse
to participate on committees. A way to cope with this problem
is to accept whatever assignments may be forthcoming and
show up for the committee meeting on time and eager to
participate. As the meeting commences, you carefully, but
surreptitiously note the first question of consequence raised in
the meeting. From then on, you listen, comment, and contribute in an exemplary manner until the meeting seems ready to

end. There is a curious phenomenon which occurs among committee members and that is that they are reluctant to end the meeting without some kind of closure or conclusion being reached even though it is quite patently only temporary. At the point where closure seems imminent, you ask the same question which was asked at the start of the meeting. By this time, everyone else will have forgotten that the question was even raised so it will have the effect of introducing a new issue just as it seemed the committee was in accord. This will cause members of the committee to feel quite uncomfortable, but they generally will not know just why, although they will vaguely associate it with you somehow. After two or three such apparently innocent performances, the word will get around that you are not a very good committee member. No one will seem to know just why since you seem interested and you contribute, but somehow you don't emerge as facilitating committee work. In a short time, you will be passed over for committee assignments. Thus, instead of gaining only 6 to 7½ hours per year of free time, you stand to gain 36 days or nearly 6 weeks of free time to pursue your own work. Since the difference between becoming an effective versus an ineffective scholar often hinges on having time to do your own thing, mastering the strategies of coping is an important achievement in college professoring.

9 *Epilogue*

FROM THEIR inception colleges have been called upon to do three main things for their students: 1) transmit the cultural heritage from one generation to the next, 2) provide the opportunity for students to learn skills necessary to practice a vocation or profession, and 3) allow individuals to pursue those areas of study which enable them to develop their unique abilities to the fullest. Colleges and universities now find themselves in the uncomfortable position of having their work interpreted by different groups according to their perceptions of which function is most important to them. Parents interpret this as a mandate to nurture their children. Legislators and boards of trustees interpret this as expecting training which will prepare the next generation to carry on the professional, business, and civic functions of society. Ethnic minorities see the universities as the training ground for leaders of a social revolution who will lead their people out of the bondage of poverty, ignorance, and prejudice into the promised land of no one seems to know just what. Each group evaluates the university functions in terms of the contribution being made to the fulfillment of the goals of the group and damns or praises the observable results. Thus colleges are apt to be the victims of a bad case of historical myopia, the severity of which depends upon which group is doing the judging.

Colleges are apt to be the victims of a bad case of historical myopia

Ignorance of most of the entire two thousand years of academic tradition is more probable among those persons who make up boards of trustees and legislative budget committees than those who pursue social reform or nurture for their offspring. Since most of these officials have achieved their visibility through the channels of business, finance, or law they tend to view universities in terms of debits and credits. To effect a balance sheet some kind of product must be the end result of the process. Thus numbers become the primary medium for judging the effectiveness of the university enterprise. It is no mere happenstance that brochures describe the number of students enrolled, number of degrees granted, number of departments, school, and colleges in the university, number of acres in the campus, number of dollars in the budget, and number of football games won or lost, for these are the absolutes which allow ledger balancing. Even when gross numbers are rejected as being synonymous with good (as, for example, the best university is the one with the biggest classes), some other use of numbers is substituted in its place (as, for example, the best university is the one with the lowest faculty-student ratio). The use of numbers as descriptors makes it possible to evaluate the university in absolutist terms, thus furthering the illusion that the university is a business (albeit a strange one) whose main function is training.

Acting on this basic misassumption, a veritable army of auditor-managers have applied their techniques to nearly every facet of the university world. Surveys of the number of job openings for elementary school teachers, or aeronautical engineers, or even administrator-managers have been used as a basis for restricting enrollments so the supply being trained will be about equal to demand. In turn, the cost per credit hour for instruction for each student at every level in various programs is used to calculate the funding of budgets. Support activities such as accounting, payroll, purchasing, etc. are provided relative to the size of the rest of the university enterprise and a defensible dollar figure for the entire operation is arrived at. From these hallowed figures all other evaluations of the university are possible. The most insidious is the cost/effectiveness ratio mentioned in Chapter 2. But others are nearly as bad. Decisions about what research will be supported are often based upon whether the university can realize a substantial return from the activity rather than whether the activity is important or meaningful to the scholars involved. It is not unusual for universities to pursue, for example, biomedical or engineering research simply because buildings and equipment are easy to obtain through federal or agency funds, but to reject research on computer-based education for minority black, chicano, or Indian children because the university will not be adding to its building or equipment inventory as a spin-off from the work. Perhaps even worse than making moral decisions based upon economics rather than principle are the consequences of the accountability procedures to training. The trend toward establishing course objectives which are only in terms of behaviors that can be observed and the accompanying competency based curriculum is the most obvious. To believe that only those outcomes of instruction which are observable are important and that all behaviors can be contained in some kind of scale that measures competency is naive at best and idiotic at worst.

Treating university functions as though the university produces an absolute product which can be assessed and will then reflect the excellence of the institution may be attractive to members of the business community and other managers, but it allows little room for recognizing that the majority of things dealt with in college lead to facts and conclusions of only tentative certainty. Stated differently, the university world is made up of ideas and ideas are abstractions derived from the world of reality. They do not profess to be of the real world nor can they ever be. To attempt to assign substance to ideas so they can be cataloged along with desks, chairs, and test

The main function of the university is not training—it is discovery

tubes for inventory is to misread the chief *raison d'etre* of universities. The main function of the university is not training — it is discovery. Therefore, to judge the effectiveness of a university by the number or even the quality of the people trained in its hallowed halls is an exercise in self-deception. On the other hand to attempt to count the number of ideas produced is just as deceptive, for ideas must always be tentative, ready to be modified or discarded as new evidence or perspectives challenge their validity. Absolutes simply fit ideas badly. The real university is a climate in which fragile ideas are cultivated. Theoretically it can exist independent of buildings, grounds, or even students. It is on this basis that the university should be judged, and it is on this basis that professors should be evaluated.

Although it is well-nigh impossible to evaluate an intellectual climate, fortunately there are some interactive effects which provide something for everyone so it is not necessary to be completely prudish about how you are being evaluated. In the best democratic tradition, it is all right to compromise when it is clear that you will lose if you don't. It is virtually impossible for any person to be associated with a college campus and remain insulated from the world of ideas for long. So long as any idea is welcome on a university campus, and is tolerated until it has been properly appraised, there will be ample opportunity for each person to find those things which have meaning for him. Because of the enormity of the idea world, many students find their introduction to a university setting one of overwhelming bewilderment. Learning to sift out those ideas with personal significance from those with none is a major task, but it can be done. What this means in practical terms is that there is no better place for a person to identify his life goals than during his college years. While this is often thought of in relation to vocational activity, it applies equally well to leisure activity, political persuasion, system of values, or spiritual commitment. Furthermore, as one exam-

The real university is a climate in which fragile ideas are cultivated

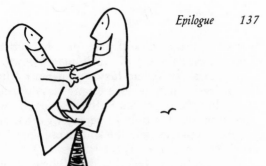
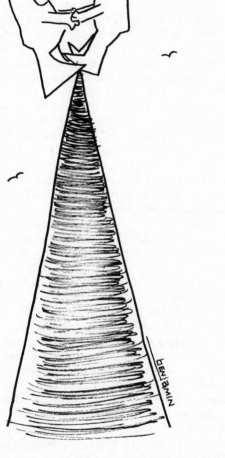

It's all right to compromise when it's clear that you will lose if you don't

ines these great ideas of past, present, and future, he is af-
forded a bird's-eye view of human history, the breadth of
human experience, and his relationship to the human condition against which he can measure his performance for the rest
of his life. Perhaps this is the real significance of a college
education, for it is only in perspective that any event can be
properly appraised and it is only from knowledge and experience that we gain perspective.

It should be obvious that it is difficult if not impossible to
maintain any sense of perspective when one is surrounded by
hysterical colleagues. From this it follows that political and
social activism are incompatible with an academic atmos-
phere. Student protests are clearly out of place on a university
campus, but they can be understood and tolerated as reflecting
the immaturity of the participants. Harassment of persons of
a persuasion different from the protestors, whether administrators, faculty, or peers, however, must not be allowed. Nor
is it proper for faculty to participate in the protest except as
they are needed to provide information or perspective to the
protestors.

It is a bit ironic that those functions upon which a university
is judged are mere by-products of the really important work
of the faculty—the pursuit of knowledge. However, it may
very well be that not being held strictly accountable for their
main work allows a great deal more flexibility to the professors since this work has not yet come under the scrutiny of
the auditor-managers. Thus while the record keepers display
their naiveté by attending to such things as the numbers of
students, buildings, departments, dollars in budgets, and won-
lost football records, the wise will judge the eminence of any
institution of higher learning on the excellence of the research
and publication activities of its professors, because this reflects
the intellectual vigor of the faculty.

So we have come full circle. Parents can indeed expect the
university to offer intellectual nurturance. Legislators and

It's difficult to maintain any sense of perspective when surrounded by hysterical colleagues

boards of trustees can expect universities to prepare the next generation to carry on the professional, business, and civic functions of society, and ethnic minorities can expect their college trained leaders to be better and wiser than those with no college training.

All this is possible because professors prefer to pursue exciting possibilities rather than to deal with humdrum realities, and the managerial types have not yet found a way to effectively monitor this activity. Perhaps we should fervently pray they never do. Prayer, however good it may make us feel, has a measurably better chance of being answered when it is backed up by action. If ninety percent of the products and practices that make civilization possible came from college and university campuses, then it is obvious that society has more than a casual stake in the continuing health and well-being of those institutions. College professors are effective precisely because they pursue highly individual goals in uniquely individual ways. By the very nature of their work they are not organized, and from intimate observation over the past twenty-five years, I have found them to be virtually unorganizable. This simply means they are terribly vulnerable to pressures from outside, particularly those which represent financial support and/or a threat to job security. Since the faculty cannot protect themselves they must be protected by others. With civilization itself hanging in the balance, everything possible must be done to assure that no individuals, groups, parties, institutions, theologies, or philosophies dictate what subjects are proper spheres for study and discussion. In addition to the freedom to explore there must also be the freedom to let that study take whatever form seems reasonable to the scholar doing the work. Only one mandate should be tolerated and that is the obligation to make the discoveries public whether they be popular or not with no fear of reprisal for subject, form, or findings — only for breach of integrity.

As with most other things in academia the actual existence

of such freedoms and protections is not always consonant with reality. Yet, as with most other things in academia, it is the pursuit of goals which sustains the institution. Perhaps this is all that can be expected — not that academic freedom will always be operative, but that some people will care enough about the future to get excited whenever academic freedom is in jeopardy. So long as that condition obtains, professors will be able to continue to do their peculiar best most of the time, and that is what this book is all about.

Index